Praise for
Mindfulness through the Stars

"If you are an astrology lover and love honesty, this book is for you. You can tell Ashley took her time catering to each sign by giving them the proper guidelines to understand not only themselves but others, too!"

—**Girls of Aqua**, astrologer and Youtuber

"Ashley speaks about astrology and the zodiac signs so intuitively! Her writing style is very down-to earth and relatable, that it makes it feel as though she's right there beside you, guiding you. She has such an amazing gift of distilling complex information into binge-worthy content. A must-read if you're on the path to self-awareness!"

—**Tati Petkovic**, astrologer, poet, and entrepreneur

"Reading this book brought a lot of insight about astrology. It's a good read since it brings knowledge and understanding in different aspects: the good, the bad, and the ugly. It's one of those books that make you want to keep reading and learn more!"

—**Brenda Rivas**, *Becoming Love* podcast

"This book has allowed me to dig into the darkest parts of myself and through the use of Ashley's questions and prompts, I've been able to heal and guide myself through my own zodiac journey!"

—**Sofia Notte**

"As someone who was only curious about astrology, Ashley's book has turned me into a believer. Her approach to sharing what a lot of people would consider boring was exceptional, which made it easy to digest and learn from. Not only does she help you understand yourself, she also does a great job of helping you work and accept yourself, which is huge as young adults. I'd recommend this book for fellas, and yes, I'm a man and I loved it."

—Shingirai Mazengwe, artist and photographer

"As someone who has studied astrology and performed these readings numerous times, Ashley brings a refreshing contemporary perspective into the zodiac signs and makes them relatable and nuanced for anyone who loves astrology. She beautifully synthesizes the core principles of astrology and mindfulness and it's a joy to read for beginners and veterans alike."

—Raven Rose, astrologer and psychic

"A very unique, intuitive, and relatable experience for self-exploration. It's a must for anyone interested in self-improvement, whether you are knowledgeable about zodiac signs or it's your first time."

—Yousef Ajameih

"I'm obsessed! Those who love astrology already and those wanting to learn will love this book. Highly recommend for anyone wanting to dig deeper within themselves and willing to do the work to reach their highest potential."

—Kahlen Barry, astrologer and YouTuber

MINDFULNESS THROUGH THE STARS

MINDFULNESS THROUGH THE STARS

A Zodiac Wellness Guide

ASHLEY FLORES

Founder of *The Amateur Guru* Youtube Channel

CORAL GABLES

Cover Design: Elina Diaz
Cover Photo/illustration: MioBuono/adobestock.com
Author photo by Shingirai Mazengwe
Layout & Design: Elina Diaz

For permission requests, please contact the publisher at:
Mango Publishing Group
2850 S Douglas Road, 2nd Floor
Coral Gables, FL 33134 USA
info@mango.bz

For special orders, quantity sales, course adoptions and corporate sales, please email the publisher at sales@mango.bz. For trade and wholesale sales, please contact Ingram Publisher Services at customer.service@ingramcontent.com or +1.800.509.4887.

Mindfulness through the Stars: A Zodiac Wellness Guide

Library of Congress Cataloging-in-Publication number: Has been requested
ISBN: (print) 978-1-64250-311-1, (ebook) 978-1-64250-312-8
BISAC category code: OCC009000—BODY, MIND & SPIRIT / Astrology / Horoscopes

Printed in the United States of America

Table of Contents

$\mathcal{A}$CKNOWLEDGMENTS

I remember the day that I truly discovered astrology. I guess you could say it was the day my life changed. I just didn't become aware of it for years to come.

It was fall 2010. I had just started a new semester of high school with my best friend Z by my side. Upon entering my first class of the day, I spotted *him*. High school me thought it was love at first sight. He had the same haircut as Justin Bieber, and that was enough for me to think we were meant to be together. To save myself from any embarrassment, we can call this high school guy Justin.

Z and I were in love with him. We wanted to get to know him, but were too insecure and shy to make the first move. So what did we do? We looked up his zodiac sign. At this time, Facebook was the most relevant form of social media, and thankfully, teenagers loved sharing way too much information on there. We looked up Justin's Facebook account, and lucky for us, right under the "about me" tab, his birthday was there for the world to see.

We looked up his sign, and according to the website, he was caring, sensitive, shy, loving, and affectionate. Then I did the next best thing and looked up my zodiac sign to see how compatible we were, and I ended up falling into the rabbit hole that is astrology. I ended up reading all about my sign (Aquarius) and the zodiac signs of every single person in my life. I was intrigued by the accuracy and couldn't stop reading.

I began skipping to the end of magazines to read the horoscope section, downloading every single astrology app available to me on my iPod touch, and asking every single person their zodiac sign! The more I studied astrology, the more I realized how much I could use this information to learn more about myself and others, and use this to my benefit! Fifteen-year-old me definitely didn't think I'd be running a YouTube channel, merchandise line, or writing a book on astrology one day, but here I am! And who knows, maybe if it wasn't for Justin and Z, I would've never thought to look up zodiac signs. So, shoutout to you guys, I guess!

I'm going to try and keep this short and sweet.

Pursuing a career that revolves heavily around astrology is not where I thought my life would go, but I'm happy it did. I come from Jamaican and Salvadorian roots, where any metaphysical concept can be quite frowned upon. Astrology is definitely not something that I was familiar with growing up. We stayed away from any sort of taboo topics. I remember one time I went to a psychic convention filled with astrologers, tarot readers, and psychics of all sorts. I came home and told my parents, and they were NOT happy.

If anyone else reading this grew up around strict, traditional parents, you understand the struggle of having withhold certain sides of yourself. Other than with Z, I never really had a chance to talk about astrology. I would ask people their zodiac signs, but the conversation never really got much deeper than that.

It wasn't until 2017, when I started my YouTube channel (*The Amateur Guru*) that I had the chance to dive deeply into the world of astrology. I found a community of people like myself on the internet to bond with over zodiac signs! Every day, I would check my notifications and see other beautiful black women like myself getting excited over zodiac signs! Coming from an all-white area, it was very cool to see girls who looked like me were engaging with my content and sharing similar interests. It pushed me to go further, and work even harder! I received so much support from my community, and I even had people messaging me, telling me that I saved their relationship, or helped them understand themselves better. It felt amazing to be able to impact someone's life; so, for that I am so thankful.

Lastly, I am so grateful to all the people in my life that contributed to help make this happen.

To my father, mother, sisters, and Tia—it is already a given—I love you, and I am grateful for all your support and wisdom. I know my rebellious Aquarian personality can worry you sometimes, but I'm sure I'll make you proud one day.

To Z, the Scorpio, thank you for showing me that not all Scorpios are evil. Sorry I told that awful story one time about your zodiac sign back when I started my astrology content. You didn't deserve that.

To A, the Pisces. You taught me that when people show me who they are, I should believe them. Thank you for that.

Thank you to my best friend, Monika, for being the prime example of a Libra for all my videos. If there is one sign I know inside out, it's the Libra. Your patience is what keeps us friends. Sorry for always calling your sign annoying. Love you.

To K, the Aquarius, thanks for showing me parts of myself that I didn't know existed, and for inspiring me everyday. I know you hate when we get sappy, but I love you.

To S, the Virgo, my heart had to be broken in order for it to open, so thank you. You've shown me my potential. I couldn't forget you even if I tried.

I'm crying now, so how about we just get this book started? We Aquarians don't deal with emotions well.

Introduction

How Astrology Can Change Your Life, and How to Get the Most from This Book

I used to think astrology was a whole lot of bullshit. I never really took the time to truly understand what it was before Z happened. Little did I know, I was depriving myself of information that I could use to my advantage. Information that I could use to better my relationship with myself, and others. Most importantly, information that I could use to improve my mental state and well-being.

Once I took the time to truly dive into the world of astrology, I was able to uncover parts of myself I didn't realize existed. Through simple research on my zodiac sign (Aquarius), I was able to understand myself through astrology just by looking at my sun sign. And I discovered there is so much more to your zodiac than just your sun sign!

Getting deeper into astrology, I learned that each person is made up of a multitude of signs. Three of the most important signs include the sun sign (your main zodiac sign), moon sign (inner emotions), and ascendant or rising sign (outer personality). Once I learned what these are, I was able to understand myself on a whole new level, and I was able find inner peace once I realized that I was not alone.

Through astrology, I uncovered many parts of myself (good, bad, and ugly), and eventually, I discovered that there are many people just like me. It was reassuring to know that there are many other Aquarians that are hypocrites, such as myself. There are many other Cancer risings who come off as snobby upon first impressions. And there are many other Virgo moons who are as critical as I am. I can't speak for everyone, but I would say there is a lot of comfort in knowing that there are other people who go through the same things as you. But most importantly, there is also power in knowing who you are.

As I learned about my sun sign, I got closer to knowing who I am. I feel as though astrology helped me piece together certain aspects of myself that I hadn't really considered. I remember the first time I read about the Aquarius sun sign; I sat at the computer for hours and kept saying, "Ahhh that explains why I'm so[insert Aquarius trait here]." I knew I was stubborn and prideful, but I never really understood why! Reading about my sign helped me understand myself better. Once I learned why I am the way I am, I was able to reflect and heal certain aspects of myself! Believe it or not, astrology is kind of like a cheat code to self-discovery. I don't want to get your hopes up too high though; a cheat code does not mean *easy way out*. Self-discovery is never easy; however, astrology can put you on the right path to begin your journey to yourself.

In this book, you will notice that each chapter (and thus zodiac sign) is divided into six sections:

✧ Self-Awareness
✧ Zodiac Signs Unlocked: The Good
✧ Zodiac Signs Unlocked: The Bad
✧ Zodiac Signs Unlocked: The Ugly
✧ Digging Deeper...
✧ Where Do I Begin?

Each section dives deeper into yourself; however, it all begins with self-awareness. It's important that you pay close attention to the self-awareness section, as that will unlock your mind, so that you can gain more out of this book. Don't get me wrong though, every section is crucial. They are all important to achieving mindfulness in their own ways. I understand these titles probably mean nothing to you right now, but don't worry! I got you. Below you will find out what to expect from each section provided to you in your zodiac signs chapter, and how to use it to your benefit.

What Is Self-Awareness and Why Do I Need It?

What on earth is self-awareness? Well, to put it simply; having self-awareness is knowing who you are. Knowing your emotions, strengths, weaknesses, likes, dislikes, desires, and motivations are all major indicators of self-awareness. People that are self-aware are able to separate themselves from the outside world. They can look at themselves as an individual, and truly evaluate who they are without the opinions of others. They are aware of how people perceive them, but remain true to themselves.

Have you ever put an outfit on and loved it so much, but then asked your friend for their opinion? They say they don't like it, so you change. Five minutes ago, you loved this outfit, but now, you doubt yourself. This is a perfectly simple example of someone who is not self-aware. If you are self-aware, look in the mirror and love what you see, no one can tell you otherwise. You might take an opinion into consideration, but it doesn't change how you see yourself. Why? *Because you know yourself.*

Practicing self-awareness is not easy. However, astrology does make it a lot easier. (Don't worry—we will get there; I just want you to understand what it is first). When you become self-aware, you have gotten to know yourself. Getting to know you is beautiful and painful all at once. You get to know all the parts of yourself that you will fall in love with, while also discovering parts of yourself that need major inner work and improvement. It's all a part of your self-love and mindfulness journey. It may seem useless or unimportant, and I get that; however, it is crucial.

Think of it this way: you're dating someone new. By date number two, are you in love? No, of course not (I mean, unless you're a hopeless romantic Pisces—then maybe you are.). How can you be in love with someone you don't even know? You have to spend a lot of time with this person. You have to figure them out. Their traumas, their passions, likes, dislikes, and more. You have to get to know this person before you can even think about love. The same thing applies to us. How can you love yourself when you barely know yourself? It is not easy. It will hurt. You will learn a lot about yourself that you are not proud of, but with that will come all the good. It's difficult, but it is worth it. It is crucial to your growth. Before you begin your journey to mindfulness, I want you to ask yourself:

Am I self-aware?

If the answer is an instant yes, congrats! You're one step ahead. If you have to think about it, you're probably not. But that's OK. That's why I'm here. Now, you might be wondering, what does this have to do with astrology? Remember when I said that astrology is like a cheat code? What if I also told you that by knowing your sun, moon, and rising signs, you can get to know yourself a little faster? By using astrology, you can ask yourself the appropriate questions to get a deeper look into your personality.

In this chapter, I suggest you grab a journal, a piece of paper, or open up the notes app on your phone. To make things a little easier for you, I'm going to provide you with a list of questions to ask yourself based on some key traits of each zodiac sign. Ask yourself these questions, write down the answers, and at the end of this book, do it all over again and see your growth. (Don't worry—I will remind you.)

For these questions, I want you to keep your moon sign in mind. Your moon sign is your inner self. It reveals the real you. The "you" that maybe only you know. It is hidden behind the mask of your ascendant sign, and dives deeper into yourself than even your sun sign. Your moon sign represents your emotions, inner thoughts, and your private self. In order to know your moon sign, you must know your birthdate, time, and place of birth. If you don't know your moon sign, there is a chart at the back of this book that will help you find it. If you have no way of knowing your time of birth, don't worry, these will still apply to your sun sign; however, they may not resonate as heavily as your moon sign might. Find your sign in this book, and ask yourself the questions provided to you in your chapter. I suggest using your sun or moon sign for best results. Reflect on the questions, and answer them as honestly as possible. And remember, these questions are not here to stroke your ego. The truth hurts, but we must face it.

Aries ♈

✧   Am I aware of how I make others feel around me, whether it is good or bad? Or am I only worried about myself?

✧   Do I feel need to be in control of every situation around me? Including things beyond my control, such as my emotions?

✧   Do I think before acting?

✧   Am I selfish?

Taurus ♉

✧ Do I manipulate situations around me to appear as a victim, knowing that this can all be avoided if I express how I feel inside?

✧ Do I believe that I am better than others?

✧ Am I stubborn and incapable of admitting when I am wrong, or do I always find a justifiable reason for my actions?

✧ Am I a lazy procrastinator?

Gemini ♊

✧ Does everyone that has experienced me know a different version of me?

✧ Do I find a problem in every solution?

✧ Do I project my internal anger onto others?

✧ Do I feel better about myself when I put others down?

Cancer ♋

✧ Do I set myself up for disappointment by expecting too much out of other people?

✧ When I am hurt, do I internalize it and wait for others to notice (and get angry/upset if they don't)?

✧ Am I genuine in my actions, or do I expect reciprocity?

✧ Do I hold grudges, and do I want to cause worse pain to those who have hurt me?

Leo ♌

✧ Am I intimidated by people who are more successful than me?

✧ Do I allow others to take advantage of my generosity out of "love"?

✧ Do I believe that I am better than everyone around me?

✧ Is my constant need to show others my greatness rooted in insecurity?

Virgo ♍

✧ Do I put too much pressure on myself and others to be perfect, and set unrealistic expectations which often lead to disappointment?

✧ Do I act out of emotion or logic?

✧ Is my way the only way, or am I able to be understanding of others?

$\diamond$ Am I stubborn? If so, how does this affect my relationship with others and myself?

Libra ♎

$\diamond$ Do I allow others to mistreat me because I want to avoid confrontation?

$\diamond$ Do I manipulate others around me to get what I want?

$\diamond$ Am I too open with people who don't deserve to have access to my inner self? If so, does this affect me or my relationships?

$\diamond$ Do I shut my loved ones out when I am upset/angry?

Scorpio ♏

$\diamond$ Do I carry my past and/or traumas into relationships with others?

$\diamond$ Am I a toxic partner/friend/family member? Do I have toxic tendencies?

$\diamond$ Do I push people away when I need them the most?

$\diamond$ Am I able to open up and be vulnerable with at least one person other than myself?

Sagittarius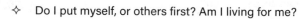

- ✧ Do I have anger issues or project my internal anger on to my loved ones who don't deserve it?

- ✧ Do I fear responsibility due to my fear of giving up my freedom?

- ✧ Do I put myself, or others first? Am I living for me?

- ✧ Do I bottle up all my emotions?

Capricorn ♑

- ✧ Do I have a fear of asking for help, even when I need it?

- ✧ Am I selfish with others?

- ✧ Am I too critical of others and myself?

- ✧ Do I believe that my way is the only/best way to do things, no matter the circumstances?

Aquarius ♒

- ✧ Am I ever able to see my wrongs, or am I too self-interested?

- ✧ Am I a hypocrite? How does this affect my relationships?

- ✧ Do I feel as though the world revolves around me, and that everyone should stop what they are doing to cater to me?

✧ Am I reactive? Do I think before I speak, or am I always out to defend myself?

Pisces ♓

✧ Am I truly misunderstood, or do I fail to even attempt to give people the chance to understand me?

✧ Do I put as much love into myself as I do into others?

✧ Am I ignorant to what is going on around me because I want to live in a state of bliss?

✧ Does anyone truly know me?

These questions, and the ones provided in each chapter, are specifically targeted toward the negative traits of each zodiac sign. Asking yourself these questions will force you to face the harsh truths of what your reality may be. Ponder them and be honest with yourself. If you answer yes to any of these questions, pay close attention to "Zodiac Signs Unlocked: The Bad." In this section, these questions will be explored, and you will be provided with healing practices, and steps to improving the flawed areas of your zodiac sign. Now, in order to achieve a greater sense of self-awareness, consider the following questions. These are simple questions that will force you to think about your inner self on a deeper level.

1. Who am I?
2. What do I like/dislike?

3.   What are my strengths/weaknesses?
4.   When am I the happiest?
5.   What is my purpose?
6.   What are my goals?
7.   How would my friends describe me?
8.   Am I proud of who I am currently?
9.   What are my goals?
10.   What areas of my life need improvement?

Grab a journal, and get writing. Put your favorite instrumental beats on YouTube, light a candle, and get to know yourself with the same eagerness you would have trying to get to know someone on a first date. Seriously. The answers don't have to be extremely profound. Keep it simple. The important thing is that you are being true to yourself in your answers. Maybe you don't want to admit you're selfish. I know I didn't. For the longest time I kept saying I just "have selfish tendencies." But the truth of the matter is, I was selfish. With my friends, family, and even myself. When I finally came to terms with this, I was able to make a change.

Another way to think of self-awareness is by comparing your current state to a car. How on earth are you supposed to fix your car if you don't know what's broken? Sure, some light on your dashboard is on, but what specifically needs attention? You need to run a diagnostic, and figure that out before any work can be done. It's not enough to know there's something wrong with you. Figure out your toxic or flawed traits, and get to work. No one can do the inner work but you, so what are you waiting for?

By now, hopefully, you understand the concept of self-awareness. I understand it can be difficult to know where to begin your journey to mindfulness. Here's where I come in. I'm going to help you discover yourself, and to become more aware, by using your zodiac sign. In your zodiac sign chapter, we'll be focusing on the best methods to discover your true self. I suggest you keep your sun and moon sign in mind. Get ready to get to know yourself on a whole new level!

Zodiac Signs Unlocked: The Good

This section is going to be all about stroking your ego. Hopefully, you have already done some work on becoming self-aware. However, if not, this section will go over some positive personality traits in your zodiac sign that you may not have realized you have, so that you can become more aware. Maybe you are unaware of the fact you're a loving and considerate person, but after reading up on your sign, you will embrace the positive qualities within you. Before we dive deeper into who you are, it is important to know the difference between a cardinal, fixed, and mutable sign (otherwise known as modalities). Each of these qualities operates differently, so it can be very helpful to understand what quality you have. At the beginning of each zodiac subsection, you will be reminded of which of the three you are.

Cardinal

Aries, Cancer, Libra, Capricorn

They are known as the leaders. Fun fact: every single cardinal zodiac sign opens a new season. Aries leads into the springtime, summer begins during Cancer season, the arrival of autumn is during Libra season, and winter begins in Capricorn. Cardinal signs are self-motivated, and are not afraid to take initiative in any given situation. They are trendsetters, and they are born leaders.

Mutable

Gemini, Virgo, Sagittarius, Pisces

Every season ends with a mutable sign. Mutable signs are more open to change. They are able to adapt to any situation. They are very helpful in assisting others in times of change. They view life from a variety of different perspectives, so they are always prepared for what is to come.

Fixed

Leo, Scorpio, Aquarius

Fixed signs are known to be more stubborn and set in their ways. They are usually aware of their purpose in life, and are able to achieve many goals because of their ability to hold steady in life, and in their goals. They have a hard time adjusting to change, and much of their personality is set from birth. They are reliable, and stable.

Now that you are aware of your modality, you can figure out how this relates to your personality. If you resonate with it, keep it in the back of your mind while reading about your sign.

Zodiac Signs Unlocked: The Bad

This will be a very brief section that will go in depth on the not-so-favorable traits of each zodiac sign. For example, the small habits that may annoy others. This will touch on the negative traits that can be annoying, but not too harmful, to you or others. Pay attention to this section if you need insight as to what some of your negative traits may be. You can use the points discussed in this section as a journal prompt, so that you may reflect on these traits and decide whether or not you resonate with them.

Zodiac Signs Unlocked: The Ugly

This section will seem simple, but it is crucial. It will focus on the main toxic trait of each zodiac sign. These toxic traits are likely to affect relationships, productivity, and one's mental state. This section is important because it reveals a side of your zodiac sign that you may not have considered. Here, you can learn how these traits might potentially be making a huge impact on your life if you were not aware of them.

Digging Deeper...

Now that you are self-aware, this section will focus on what to do with the information provided to you in this book. This section will go over how everything you discovered about yourself could potentially be affecting your relationships with others. Once you read this part, if it resonates with you, you will be more mindful of these traits when interacting with others.

Where Do I Begin?

This section will be short and sweet. How can you begin to break these habits? How can you use this information to better yourself and become the evolved version of your zodiac sign? In this section, you will be provided with techniques and self-reflection questions on how to deal with issues with others based off your zodiac sign.

CHAPTER 1

The Aries

March 21-April 19

Ruling planet: Mars ♂ **Element:** Fire △ **Symbol:** Ram ♈
Quality: Cardinal **Opposite sign:** Libra

Self-Awareness

As an Aries, you might be having trouble in getting to know your flaws. Most Aries I've come across are overly confident, and a little blind to their own weaknesses. I've had many Aries friends that are constantly arguing with their loved ones, but refuse to see that they might be the problem.

One of my overly confident friends (we'll name her Joanna for the sake of this book) used to constantly ask me for relationship advice. Being the honest Aquarius that I am, I had no issue letting Joanna know when she was in the wrong. The problem was, no matter what I would say, Joanna came up with an excuse. She could not accept that the root of most of her relationship problems began with her, so she never did the inner work on herself to be better! Instead, she ended up in multiple relationships that led nowhere.

Don't be discouraged though. If you've picked up this book, you are ready to do the inner work. I believe in you! In my opinion, every sign has their own unique way of becoming more aware. Some methods might be similar (probably signs within the same elements). However, I'm here to give you a personalized self-awareness guide.

Step 1: Ask your most trusted friend or family member to name ten of your best and worst traits

As an Aries, the opinions of others matter a lot to you. If you were to sit down, look in the mirror, and ask yourself to come up with ten bad traits, you would probably find only one. That's okay (I wish I had that confidence, but my overly critical Virgo moon gets in the way). This is why we have our loved ones around. To tell us the shit we don't want to hear. You just have to be willing to listen. I suggest asking a few friends, just to see if there is a pattern. If five friends tell you you're selfish, I think it's a good idea to reflect on that. If four people say you're considerate, then you probably are.

Step 2: Make a list of all the good and bad traits your loved one made you aware of

Again, you're allowed to disagree, just make sure you are fair to yourself, and take the time to reflect on the traits your loved ones have given you. If they say you're selfish and you do not resonate with this, ask them why they said this. Ask for examples. Don't stop there. Get as much information as you can, so that you can get to the truth. Maybe after a few conversations, you will realize that you *are* selfish. You are also human, and humans are not perfect. Now that you know you possess certain negative traits, you can work on them! You ran the diagnostic, and now you can start fixing your car!

Step 3: Document your process on video

As an Aries, you probably have a busy life. You like to get things done quickly and be productive. Normally, I suggest journaling (that's what I do), but I can't help but think you would prefer a less time-consuming method. Instead, grab your smartphone and do a weekly check-in. Document your progress on this journey. Talk about what you have learned about yourself, what you are working on, the progress, and how you feel. Answer some of the earlier questions on video, and re-watch them at the end of the month to see how far you have come. You might see progress in two weeks, or four months! There is no timeline. Don't rush this process. This is your mental health! It's okay if it takes time. Make these videos one to five minutes in length, and start to see how much your life will change! If videos do not work for you, keep notes on your phone and make sure they are dated. Whatever works for YOU!

Step 4: Hold yourself accountable by telling a friend about your journey

You probably fear failure. If you are only accountable to yourself, it is more likely that you may neglect your self-awareness journey. If you tell a loved one about the work you are doing to improve your mental health, it holds you accountable. If you decide it's too much, or you can't keep up with the inner work, you probably don't want to tell someone else you've given up. How embarrassing. If someone else knows about your process, it will help to keep you on this path. And remember, you are doing this for YOU! So lying to a friend when they ask you if you recorded your progress or wrote in your journal last night isn't going to help anyone. You got this!

Zodiac Signs Unlocked: The Good

You know those people that you meet who you can't seem to find anything wrong with? It's almost like they can do no wrong. They're personable, funny, charming, and couldn't hurt a fly. Yeah, they're probably Aries. Upon first impressions, Aries are one of the friendliest signs. They are talkative and charming, and know how to keep a conversation going (sometimes for too long). If you are an Aries, you probably consider yourself to be the best person in the room, no matter the who is in it. Especially, if your rising sign is Aries. Your exterior appearance will come off as confident, unbothered, and loving. That's the type of energy I think we could all benefit from. The typical Aries (sun, moon, or rising) may display some of the following traits:

Sun: Leadership abilities, practical, confident, risk-taker, efficient, open, productive

Moon: Outspoken, loving, considerate, sensitive, caring, nurturing

Rising: Energetic, talkative, courageous, funny, flirty, open, charming, personable

The Evolved Aries

The evolved Aries is like no other. That is what we are trying to achieve through this book, to evolve, and become the greatest version of ourselves. If you practice the methods given to you in this book, you can and will become your best self! As an evolved Aries, you will experience confidence inside and out. The Aries radiates confidence like no other. Once you reach this point, everywhere you talk, you will grab the attention of others. People will want to know you, or be you—but they won't know why. It's the energy that you give off as an evolved Aries. This Aries is also kind and selfless.

I remember being super close to an Aries named Ciara for many years. Ciara was one of the most selfless persons I've ever known. She was the type to give you her last dollar. Seriously. I remember for my birthday one year, she used her last fifty dollars to buy me a gift, even though I told her not to. This may not sound like a big deal to some, but Ciara was in no position to be spending any kind of money. She had no job, and parents who did not financially support her. However, she still chose to spend her last bit of money on her close friend. We don't talk anymore, but I will never forget that. That was the first time I had witnessed a selfless Aries. Contrary to popular belief, they do exist!

It is a common trait in Aries to be extremely selfish, however, that is an immature Aries. Aries are actually extremely selfless with the ones they love. They put others before them, and make sure that the people they love and care for are happy. They are extremely loving, kind, and nurturing. Outside of their personal relationships, they are extremely driven and courageous. They know what they want, and they will stop at nothing to get it. They are in an ongoing competition with themselves which leads them to constantly strive for greatness. I have never met an unsuccessful evolved Aries. I don't even think they exist. The evolved Aries is motivated and inspired. They usually take on many projects, and are able to give each one their full attention. In their work life, they gladly take on leadership roles, as they love to be in charge. Aries are great with time management, and are extremely efficient. They know how to get things done FAST! It's like their life is constantly on fast forward. Seriously. They do everything fast. Cooking, working, talking, hell—they even fall in love fast!

Zodiac Signs Unlocked: The Bad

As mentioned, Aries is one of those signs that appears perfect upon first impression. They seem like the most personable, friendly, and hardworking people you will ever meet. They definitely can be; however, the unevolved Aries carries many negative personality traits as well. Where there is good, there is always bad. If you are an Aries, I suggest you make the effort be more mindful of some of your less favorable traits. I have provided you with some traits that shouldn't be considered a big deal, however, these traits can affect your relationships with others without you even realizing it.

Bossy: As an Aries, you love to be in charge. In most situations, you are likely to take the lead. However, make sure you know the difference between taking the lead, and taking over. Many Aries love to be in a position of power. Unfortunately, it is common for Aries to abuse that power. An unevolved Aries is likely to take control over any situation, because they enjoy bossing others around. This often occurs in work environments, and romantic relationships. In most partnerships, the Aries is likely to be the one "wearing the pants." This can be OK, just make sure you don't let any position of power get to your head.

Hot Tempered: Many Aries have an extremely quick temper. When they are happy, they are some of the most loveable people in the world. However, they can get very temperamental. Their anger is like no other. They can explode within a matter of minutes. Anyone in his or her path will face the wrath of an Aries, and it is not pretty. The problem about the Aries temper is that usually, it is completely irrational. They do not take the time to think before reacting. Oftentimes, they *overreact*, and tend to say things they do not mean. They get over situations as quickly as they react, but at that point, the damage has been done.

Reckless: Aries can be extremely reckless. They make very rash decisions, without thinking them through. They do not always put themselves first. If you are an Aries, you will probably find yourself in a lot of problematic situations that you could have avoided. Whether you jumped in a relationship too quickly, accepted a job offer that you didn't think through, or maybe even did something as extreme as signing a contract you didn't read. Aries are known for their reckless behavior, and rash decisions! Be careful Aries; some things can't be undone.

Zodiac Signs Unlocked: The Ugly

The toxic trait you need to be aware of: Oblivion to your affect on others

How this affects my...

Relationships: You have a hard time seeing when you are in the wrong, which causes you to hurt your loved ones without even realizing it.

Productivity: You miss out on many potential opportunities.

Mental state: When people finally open up to you about how you have affected them, it can feel like an attack, and you will get defensive.

Digging Deeper...

Toxic trait: Oblivion to your affect on others

As an Aries, you tend to live in your own little world. What you fail to realize sometimes is that other people live here too. At times, you act as though the only person who could potentially be affected by your actions is you. This happens in many different areas in life.

You have a very strong personality, so naturally, people are drawn to you. Once people get close to you, they have certain expectations as to what you will provide in the relationship, whether it be platonic, romantic, or even work relationships. Because of your friendly personality, people will feel closer to you than they really are. They will have high expectations, but will be let down because you are not making them a priority. You might view them as an acquaintance, but in their mind, you are close friends.

As an Aries, it is important that you become very intentional with your relationships. Once you realize who someone is to you, make it truly clear. This will be beneficial because people will have more realistic expectations when dealing with you, which will lead to less disappointment. If you can become more aware of this trait, you will find it much easier to view how your actions are affecting others.

Where Do I Begin?

I will tell you the same thing that I have told every single zodiac sign. Begin with the end in mind. Where do you see yourself at end of this mindfulness journey? Don't take the word "end" too seriously; this is a lifelong journey. It is important to understand where you see yourself after you have done all the crucial healing and inner work. That will keep you in alignment with your purpose. To understand your purpose, ask yourself the following three questions. These have all been customized to your moon sign. You can apply them to your sun sign as well.

1. How can I be more mindful of my effect on others?

2. What steps can I take, so that I can get into the habit of thinking before reacting?

3. How can I prioritize myself and my loved ones?

CHAPTER 2

The Taurus

April 20-May 20

Ruling planet: Venus ♀ **Element:** Earth ▽ **Symbol:** Bull ♉
Quality: Fixed **Opposite sign:** Scorpio

Self-Awareness

As a Taurus, you can be quite stubborn. Right now, you're probably reading this and thinking something along the lines of "I'm not stubborn at all, that's just an annoying Taurus stereotype." I hate to break it to you, but the fact that you can't even recognize that you might be stubborn is a huge sign that you probably are. I remember I casually dated a Taurus for a few months. He was the most stubborn person I had ever met. He would argue with me about anything and everything! I'm not joking. It was exhausting. I would teasingly make fun of him, and let him know that he didn't always have to be right, and he would get angry and insist that he already knew that, had no issue in admitting when he was wrong, and that it wasn't his fault that he always happened to be right! Needless to say, that didn't work out.

Self-awareness will probably be a little more difficult for you because it may take some time to be able to face your truths. Be patient with yourself and pay attention to the four steps customized to your sign below.

Step 1: Ask the one person you trust to give you a detailed list of all your worst traits and ask them for examples

We all have that one person that we really listen to. The one whose opinion is valued and taken into consideration, no matter how stubborn you are. It's usually someone who knows you inside out. It could be your mother or father. Maybe it's your best friend, or your significant other. Figure out who it is, and ask them to break down all your worst traits to you. Don't interrupt them, and don't get defensive. Remember, YOU asked for this. If you can't take it, then you're not ready for this journey. Write down the list and reflect.

Step 2: Find videos online or books on people with similar issues

As a Taurus, you probably need some reassurance. You're sensitive. That's OK. Go on YouTube and search for some videos on the traits you want to work on. Podcasts and books are also an option! If someone told you that you are stubborn, then there's gotta be a video out there explaining how someone overcame their selfish behavior. Grab a snack, and watch your favorite content creator go on for twenty-two minutes on how they used to be selfish. Listen to what they are saying. You'll probably resonate with a lot of points they go over, and this might even be the first time you come to recognize certain patterns and behaviors. Be open to it, and understand that you are not alone. This realization will help you on your journey.

Step 3: Monitor your reactions and behaviors to see if there are patterns

At the end of each day, sit down and reflect on your interactions that day. If you have a long commute, do this on the bus or in traffic. Allow the outside world to fall silent as you reflect on your day. Ask yourself some questions. Examples:

✧   Did I offend or upset anyone today?

✧   Did I treat the people around me fairly?

✧   Was I stubborn in any situation?

✧   Did I show affection or love to others?

These are just some examples, but if I were you, I would base my questions off the negative traits provided to me by my loved one. Every day, you will find that you are becoming more and more honest with yourself. Eventually, you will be able to recognize when you are not being your best self, and you'll start to learn how to correct your behavior.

Step 4: Practice acknowledgment when you are "acting up"

Once you can recognize when your actions are due to bad traits, you can acknowledge them. If you realize you are being insensitive with your friend mid-argument, acknowledge it. Even if you don't believe you need to apologize, acknowledge it. An example of this could be, "What I just said was inconsiderate, what I meant to say was..." Once you begin to point these moments out, you will build a habit of stopping yourself before things get bad. Eventually, you will probably stop having these moments altogether. It will take practice, control, and awareness. You must be patient with yourself, but I believe in you!

Zodiac Signs Unlocked: The Good

Tauruses are one of those signs that when you first meet them, they seem shy, but once you get to know them a little better, you realize they actually aren't shy at all. If anything, they are a little reserved upon first impressions, but they soon become extremely talkative and humorous. If you are a Taurus, you might overthink your personality sometimes. You worry about what other people think, but you really don't need to. Trust me. People like you the way you are. You really don't need to do anything extra to compensate for shortcomings, because in reality, that's what pushes people away. I've noticed that many Tauruses are extremely considerate and caring, even when they barely know you. This is what draws people to your sign. The typical Taurus (sun, moon, or rising) may display some of the following traits:

- **Sun**: Practical, dependable, stable, nurturing, careful, attentive, patient, witty

- **Moon**: Loving, nurturing, considerate, generous, kind, giving, attentive, affectionate

- **Rising**: Conservative, calm, reserved, shy/quiet, timid, constructive

The Evolved Taurus

The evolved Taurus is very special. If I am being honest, I don't meet them very often. I'm sure you know Tauruses are known to be the most stubborn sign in the zodiac. Yes, this is true. However, the evolved Taurus is much more logical. This is the version that you want to become. This Taurus is sensible and reasonable. They can see when they are in the wrong, even if they have a hard time admitting it. Of course, they are far from perfect, but if you work on yourself enough to morph into this evolved version of you, you will be amazing! Your communication skills will improve. You will find that you are getting into fewer arguments with your loved ones, and that any arguments that do occur are short-lived! You will have more love to give, and therefore will be more open to receiving love.

As a Taurus, you have a deep appreciation for the finer things in life. However, once you become the greatest version of yourself, you will have a newfound appreciation for even the little things. Your mind will be more open. Once you tap into this part of yourself, you will find that you do not feel the need to add an extra layer to your personality to please others. This is something an unevolved Taurus often does. You will become so comfortable with yourself that the opinion of others will no longer concern you. Not only that, but you will find that you have less opinions of other people.

At times, Tauruses can be quite judgmental, but with enough inner work, this can be changed (yes, even though you are a fixed sign, you CAN change). An evolved Taurus is also generous, and if you are close to them, they give with fewer expectations than the average Taurus. It may take a bit of time for the Taurus to open themselves up. However, it is worth the wait.

Zodiac Signs Unlocked: The Bad

As a Taurus, you can be one of the most loveable, yet irritating, signs all at once. You have such a great personality, but Tauruses tend to be so stuck in their ways that their bad traits can become quite annoying if you are around them too often. If you are a Taurus, I suggest you make the effort be more mindful of some of your less favorable traits. I have provided you with some characteristics that shouldn't be considered a big deal. However, these aspects can affect your relationships with others without you even realizing it.

Stubborn: If someone told you to name the first thing that comes to mind when you hear the word "Taurus," I guarantee you would say stubborn. This isn't a myth, or stereotype; this is a very real thing. Taurus are most stubborn of the zodiac. Their stubbornness causes poor communication on their end, which only makes their life harder. If you are a Taurus, work on becoming self-aware enough to understand that you are probably stubborn. It is common for Taurus to deny the fact that they are in fact, stubborn. However, that's just their stubbornness talking.

Materialistic: Many Tauruses take a liking to the finer things in life, and they can be quite materialistic. This is not always an issue; however, the unevolved Taurus can be extremely self-indulgent. Oftentimes, they will prioritize material possessions over more important things. Keeping up with a lifestyle that is beyond your means is never a good idea, Taurus. If you resonate with this, be very careful. Don't go broke trying to look rich.

Lazy: From afar, the Taurus is great at keeping up the appearance that they are constantly driven and motivated. They can be, but only if they like what they are doing. If it does not benefit them, or isn't what they love, they are not interested. Even mundane tasks such as washing dishes, taking out the garbage, and cleaning their car are chores they will avoid for as long as possible, and when they finally get to them, it's likely they will be complaining the whole time. Don't be that Taurus!

Zodiac Signs Unlocked: The Ugly

The toxic trait you need to be aware of: Being overly concerned with the opinions of others

How this affects my...

Relationships: You have a hard time being your authentic self in certain relationships. This can prevent it from progressing.

Productivity: Spending too much time worrying about what people think will stop you from going after what you truly want. You might miss opportunities because you are too concerned with what people will think.

Mental state: You will be overly critical of yourself when you worry more about others' opinions than your own. This can decrease your confidence.

Digging Deeper...

Toxic trait: Being overly concerned with the opinion of others

As a Taurus, you can be extremely critical—of yourself, and others. Because Tauruses often spend time observing others, they have this preconceived notion that everyone around them is observing and judging the same way they do. Truth is, no one really cares. Because of their ego, the Taurus is often concerned with the opinions of others. They are easily embarrassed, and sometimes have a hard time feeling comfortable in public settings, because they are worried about what people think of them.

This can affect certain relationships, if they are not paired with someone who is fully compatible with their personality. If the Taurus is very close with someone who is extroverted and carefree, they may find that they are constantly being forced out of their comfort zone to make someone else happy. Depending on the Taurus, this can build resentment and anger toward their loved ones, because they feel slightly disrespected. The Taurus is overly sensitive, so it will not take much for them to feel this way.

As a Taurus, it is important that you express when something is making you uncomfortable, so you can avoid any type of resentment or built up anger. However, getting out of your comfort zone is not necessarily a bad thing. People don't care as much as you think they do. The only one worried about what you're doing is you.

Where Do I Begin?

I will tell you the same thing that I have told every single zodiac sign. Begin with the end in mind. Where do you see yourself at end of this mindfulness journey? Don't take the word "end" too seriously; this is a lifelong journey. It is important to understand where you see yourself after you have done all the crucial healing and inner work. That will keep you in alignment with your purpose. To understand your purpose, ask yourself the following three questions. These have all been customized to your moon sign. You can apply them to your sun sign as well.

1. How can I be more open minded, so that I may see when I am in the wrong?

2. Why am I so concerned with the opinion of others, and how can I change this?

3. Is my ego getting in the way of having fulfilling relationships?

CHAPTER 3

May 21–June 20

Ruling planet: Mercury ☿ **Element:** Air △ **Symbol:** The Twins ♊
Quality: Mutable **Opposite sign:** Sagittarius

Self-Awareness

As a Gemini, you can probably see your own flaws, but lack the willingness to do anything about them. You know that you get too angry at times, but you constantly justify your behaviors. One moment, it's the right way to react, and then you realize it's not. By that point, the dust has settled, and you don't feel the need to apologize or address your negative reactions.

There was this male Gemini that I worked with for years, and whenever he was in a bad mood, he would mistreat people. We all just knew to ignore him, and not take anything personally, because he would quickly get over whatever he was angry about. One day he snapped at me for not filling something out properly (even though it was my third day on the job), then ten minutes later he was offering to buy me Starbucks! I was so confused.

Geminis have a habit of taking out their own personal issues on others, then acting as though nothing happened, because in their minds they become aware that it had nothing to do with you. This isn't fair, and it affects people around you. Trust me. It's like you have a constant internal battle in your mind over whether or not something is wrong. I'm here to tell you, you are not always right. You know this, but let it sink in. Just because you can justify your negative behaviors in the moment doesn't mean it's okay. With some self-reflection, I think you will understand yourself quite easily. You are not naïve. Sometimes, you just need that extra push.

Step 1: Try and discover your toxic/negative traits through media consumption

This might sound crazy, but here's the thing. I believe Geminis are one of the most self-aware signs. You probably have an idea of what your flaws and weaknesses are; you just haven't cared enough to work on them. When I say "discover your traits through media consumption" I mean, relate who you are to characters in your favorite shows, movies, or books. Is there a character that you feel very similar to? Every time you watch them, they remind you of yourself? The good and the bad. Pay attention to the bad!

I remember I was watching a movie called *Something Borrowed* and I realized I felt just like Kate Hudson's character, and I didn't like that at all. If you've never watched the movie (or read the book), Kate Hudson's character was very demanding, self-absorbed, and inconsiderate of her best friend's feelings. This led to her best friend feeling as though she was living in her shadow and resenting her. Eventually, her best friend had an affair with Kate Hudson's character's husband. Kate's character was very blind to this affair because she was so self-centered. She did not care about her friend's personal life, and she neglected any emotional needs. I became frustrated with myself for resonating with her so deeply, and instantly wanted to improve certain traits. Trust me. This helps! You just need to see your flaws in action from a third-person perspective.

Step 2: Once you are aware, ask people to confirm!

You can be quite indecisive at times. Practice step 1, draft a list of all the negative traits you may have discovered about yourself, and ask people around you to confirm or deny if it is the truth. Only ask people who can be blunt and honest with you. If you don't have people like that in your life, then trust your own judgment. Hold on to this list and reflect on it often.

Step 3: Remove all distractions until you can be alone in your thoughts.

As a Gemini, your mind is constantly moving. You are usually quite busy. You're not typically someone who is bored since you like to be stimulated. In my opinion, there are two types of Geminis. The chill, loner Gemini, who likes to stay in, and the social butterfly Gemini, who is constantly surrounded by others. Both Geminis know how to keep themselves entertained, therefore, there is not much time for self-reflection.

Do you ever take time to do nothing? I mean nothing at all. Remove all distractions, so that you can give yourself some time for self-reflection. Maybe even take a bubble bath, or go for a jog with no music. Let yourself think. This will give you some time for some serious soul searching.

Step 4: Figure out who you are, and pay attention to who you're not.

Usually a Gemini can be on either end of the same spectrum. For example, you can be both easy-going, but quick tempered. Pay attention to both sides. Work on both traits. As a Gemini, you have the whole "twin" thing going on. The two-faced zodiac sign. This is a real thing, and this might mean you have to put a little more work in once you've discovered yourself a bit more. It may seem like a lot, but it is possible. I believe in you!

Zodiac Signs Unlocked: The Good

It there is one sign in the zodiac that is unfazed by the opinions of others, it's the Gemini. Every Gemini I've ever come across (even the insecure ones) couldn't care less about what people think. It's honestly inspiring. I've never met a sign that is so self-assured. You know that phone voice you turn on when you pick up the phone and it's your employer? It's similar to that customer service voice you put on if you've ever worked retail. Most Geminis don't have that. They are 100 percent themselves the moment you meet them. They can't be bothered to put on a façade, whether you like them or not. Gemini's are one of the craziest signs you'll ever meet, and you will learn that very quickly. You will either love them, or hate them for it. I personally love them for it, but I understand why they are not everyone's cup of tea. The typical Gemini (sun, moon, or rising) may display some of the following traits:

- **Sun:** Entertaining, youthful, energetic, stimulating, funny, full of surprises, loving, loyal, interesting

- **Moon:** Bright, communicative, adaptable, loving, affectionate, confident

- **Rising:** Charming, witty, caring, entertaining, crazy, outgoing, personable, carefree

The Evolved Gemini

A Gemini that is evolved is one of the best signs to be around. Their energy is contagious. They know how to enjoy life, and won't let anything get in the way of that. They love making new friends, but they can also appreciate their solitude. I usually come across two different types of Geminis: the reserved, loner Gemini, and the outgoing/extroverted Gemini. Don't get it confused though, the loner one isn't shy; they just prefer a laidback setting. Both Geminis are extremely stimulating. They are always ready for a deep conversation with no judgement. They are carefree, and their energy is extremely magnetic.

An evolved Gemini is not afraid to step out of their comfort zone, if they know it will benefit them. They can be very fearless, and therefore, they are able to achieve many goals. There is a huge difference between an unevolved vs. an evolved Gemini. If you are a Gemini that is evolving, you will notice that you are not easily phased anymore. Many Geminis are known for their quick tempers, and for overreacting, but once you get to a higher vibration, you will realize that many things are not worth your energy. You will become a more rational, and fairer version of yourself. Your communication skills will improve, and you will be more aware of your toxic behaviors. The Gemini is an extreme overthinker, so you may become a little more critical of yourself. Make an effort to be self-aware, yet realistic about whom you are becoming. Do not strive for perfection, or it will lead to unhappiness. Don't worry though, you are a mutable sign, so there is definitely room for improvement and change!

Zodiac Signs Unlocked: The Bad

The Gemini is one of those signs that people can't decide whether they love them, or they hate them. It's mostly because every time you interact with one, you get a different version of them. It can be seriously confusing. If you are a Gemini, I suggest you make the effort be more mindful of some of your less favorable traits. I have provided you with some traits that shouldn't be considered a big deal, however, these traits can affect your relationships with others without you even realizing it.

Gossipy: Many Gemini's end up getting themselves into lots of problems because they tend to gossip, A LOT. Geminis are a talkative sign, and many of their conversations end up being about other people. They do not gossip with malicious intent; however, it can come across this way when received by the wrong person. If you are a Gemini who tends to gossip, be very aware of the people you are speaking to and whether or not they can be trusted. I know you don't mean harm, but sometimes, your words can come off as insensitive. My suggestion? Stop talking about people in general. You'll feel better. Trust me.

Attention seeking: Geminis love to be the center of attention. If you look back to your high school days (or if you're currently in high school, ask around), you'll notice that many of the "popular kids" had summer birthdays, usually during Gemini season. Geminis have a way of becoming the center of attention (unless a Leo is in the room) and they live for it! The problem is that at times, they go a little too far for attention, and it's not usually worth it.

Irritable: The Gemini is a very impatient sign. They are quick-tempered, and get irritated very easily. When you're around a Gemini, you will find yourself walking on eggshells around them to avoid conflict. You will bite your tongue often, knowing that one wrong sentence can set them off. If you are a Gemini who resonates with this, try your hardest to rationalize your thoughts before snapping at someone who probably doesn't deserve it.

Zodiac Signs Unlocked: The Ugly

The toxic trait you need to be aware of: Dual personality

How this affects my...

Relationships: People often have a hard time getting close to you, because they feel as though they never truly know you.

Productivity: You change your lifestyle often because of your ever-changing moods. It is likely that you change jobs frequently, or jump into relationships because you get bored so easily. Progression is slow for you because you are constantly starting over.

Mental state: Getting to know your self and becoming self-aware is more difficult for you.

Digging Deeper...

Toxic trait: Dual personality

Geminis are very confusing because you never know which version of them you will get. All Geminis have a dual personality, whether they'd like to admit it or not. There is the sweet, charming, and loving Gemini, but there is also the angry, controlling, irritable Gemini. Because of this, people are usually confused at where their relationship with a Gemini is. One day they will feel like the closest of friends, the next day, they feel like mere acquaintances.

The Gemini runs extremely hot and cold, and doesn't realize that by being this way, they are pushing people away. It's almost as if you are constantly taking two steps forward, and one step back when entering a relationship with a Gemini. As a Gemini, it is important that you gain control over your emotions. Your mood will impact how you treat others, and you let it go too far. Try to think before reacting when you realize your mood has shifted. I understand you get bored easily, but it is important that you make the effort to keep people at a distance before getting to close to them. This way, if you change your mind about them, it won't be as confusing for the other person.

Your dual personality is sometimes difficult to be around. You are unpredictable, and confusing. Many people do not always want to stick around and wait for your mood to change, as it can be extremely frustrating. If you need time to be alone so that you can sort through your thoughts, do that. It is important that your mind is settled before you interact with others.

Where Do I Begin?

I will tell you the same thing that I have told every single zodiac sign. Begin with the end in mind. Where do you see yourself at end of this mindfulness journey? Don't take the word "end" too seriously; this is a lifelong journey. It is important to understand where you see yourself after you have done all the crucial healing and inner work. That will keep you in alignment with your purpose. To understand your purpose, ask yourself the following three questions. These have all been customized to your moon sign. You can apply them to your sun sign as well.

1. Why do I feel the need to change my personality to please others?

2. Do I crave attention? Why?

3. How can I be more patient with others?

CHAPTER 4

THE CANCER

June 21-July 22

Ruling planet: Moon ☽ Element: Water ▽ Symbol: The Crab ♋
Quality: Cardinal **Opposite sign:** Capricorn

Self-Awareness

As the Cancer that you are, I can say with confidence that many of you reading this are already pretty self-aware. You probably know a lot of your weak points and toxic behaviors. Your issue may just be "what's next?" or "I know I'm [insert toxic trait here], but that doesn't bother me. People just have to accept it." So I'm just going to come out and say it. *Just because you are OK with these traits, doesn't mean other people are.* Read that again.

A lot of you know that you have an ego the size of the moon (your ruling planet, in case you didn't know). Many of you know that you are way too forgiving, and I'm pretty damn sure a good chunk of you reading this can admit that you are way too sensitive. I've had many Cancer friends, and let me tell you, the unevolved ones are exhausting!

I had one friend who let her ego get in the way of everything she wanted in life, and instead of making the decision to work on it, she would spend her days complaining about missed opportunities! I would constantly say things like, "Casey, if you know that you're letting your pride get in the way of getting to a good relationship, why don't you just put it aside?" She would come up with a million excuses as to why that'll never be possible. "It's just who I am," she'd say, but in the same night, she would cry herself to sleep.

This self-sabotaging behavior might not seem like a big deal, but when you realize that you rarely get the things you want because of it, maybe it's time to work on it. So now what do you do with this info? Well, that's where chapter three and four come in. For now, I'm here to talk to the small percent of Cancers that lack that self-awareness. If that's you, then I'm about to give you some steps on becoming more aware. Pay attention!

Step 1: Pay attention to the moon cycles

As a Cancer, you have a deep connection to your ruling planet, the moon. For this reason, I find Cancers very lucky. You are so emotionally connected to the moon, and you can use this to your advantage more than others. Now, you may be wondering how this relates to self-awareness. If you pay attention to each phase of the moon, you can see how it affects you and your emotions. If there is a time that you want to dedicate to some serious soul-searching or self-reflection, use the phases of the moon to decide when it is time!

I highly suggest using the waning gibbous moon (better known as a crescent moon), for some inner work. This is the time that you want to pay attention to what your feeling and thinking. I say this because at certain phases of the moon, your emotions are heightened, and it is easier for you to release any energy that no longer serves you! I usually do all my deep healing at this time, or even during a new moon or full moon. If you have not already started this self-awareness journey, wait until the waning gibbous (crescent) moon!

Step 2: Journal, journal, journal

Now that you know when the best time to begin your journey, grab your journal and get to work! As a Cancer, you are constantly going through a flood of emotions and thoughts, and usually you have no emotional release. You don't open up to others easily. Grab your favorite journal, and get ready to get to know yourself on a whole new level. Remember those questions in the beginning of this chapter? The ones that probably made you feel so personally attacked that you wanted to cry? The waning gibbous moon is the best time to answer those. Be honest with yourself, and don't hold back. Dedicate three pages for one question if you need to. Now is the time to unlock your mind and dig deep.

Step 3: Re-read your entries…often!

As I mentioned, you probably already know a lot about who you are as an individual. Now that you're journaling (hopefully!), you have the chance to revisit certain parts of your brain. Seriously. It's amazing! By journaling, you can track your progress and growth.

I remember, there was a point in which I would revisit my journal entries at the end of every month, and I would be absolutely mind blown at my growth. I discovered that the things that affected me in the beginning of the month, I had forgotten about by the time I re-read my entries. I would stop caring about certain things, or I would realize I'd dropped bad habits just by reading my journals. I would have never noticed my progression if it wasn't for revisiting my journal.

Before I re-read my entries, I felt stuck! By the time I finish reading, I would be amazed with my progress and myself. This is a major key to self-awareness, and as a Cancer—I think this is the method for you. I know you don't want to open up to anyone else, so open up to yourself!

Step 4: Don't be so hard on yourself

The reason why revisiting your journal is so important to your journey is because it is reassuring. As a Cancer, you are sensitive, and require reassurance often. Seeing your progression will build confidence. Once you have that confidence, you are unstoppable! That in itself will be motivation for you to keep on going to become the best version of yourself! Just continue to stay strong in your efforts, and do not be so hard on yourself. Tell your loved ones about your self-improvement journey! They will encourage you and push you to be better. You need that push sometimes, and that's OK. Everything will work in your favor; you just have to keep going. You got this!

Zodiac Signs Unlocked: The Good

The Cancer is just one of those signs that are full of surprises. They are extremely quiet, yet social at the same time. Every time I've met one, I assume they're boring until I see them in a different environment. They adapt well in social settings, but they definitely like to analyze the setting before letting their guard down. Once a Cancer lets their guard down, they are some of the friendliest people you will ever meet. Seriously. They treat you like a close friend within minutes of meeting them, and for some reason they just feel like home. They are extremely loving and nurturing, and if you have a Cancer close to you in life, consider yourself lucky. The typical Cancer (sun, moon, or rising) may display some of the following traits:

- **Sun**: Fun, friendly, social, spunky, surprising, talkative, considerate, protective

- **Moon**: Loving, emotional, sensitive, nurturing, sweet, domesticated, helpful

↑ **Rising**: Introverted, kind, quiet, caring, familiar, charismatic, compassionate

The Evolved Cancer

A Cancer that is evolved is one of my favorite signs. They don't come with all the toxicity that another Cancer may bring to the table. They are extremely friendly and loveable. They care for you the same way a close relative or mother would. A self-aware Cancer is even better! When you come across a Cancer that is self-aware, the relationship (whether romantic or platonic) is so easy! There is less confrontation.

If you are working toward becoming an evolved Cancer, you will become one of the most loved people, no matter where you go. You are social and friendly, but you are also extremely caring and considerate. You'd give someone else the shirt off your back, and would never expect a thing in return. You also make people feel comfortable opening up to you. This is something that is very important in relationships. As a Cancer, your emotions are heightened. When you are happy, the whole world glows and everything is amazing. People are drawn to you, and your energy is magnetic.

As a Cancer, you tend to deal with a lot of mood swings. If you can take control over your emotions, and the constant energy shifts you have to deal with, you will be an unstoppable force! It is typically the Cancer's moodiness that keeps people away.

It's something that many of you don't know how to control. It is important that you learn how to work with your moods.

Being a moon child, you are sensitive and empathetic. You get along great with others because of your ability to relate so well to them. You take on the emotions of other people as your own. This can be good or bad. When this is good, it is because this enables you to grow closer bonds with other people. Usually, a Cancer has many friends, but only a select few that are close to them. When a Cancer is evolved, they are able to set fair boundaries in relationships, while still giving it their all!

Zodiac Signs Unlocked: The Bad

The Cancer is one of those signs that give you high highs, and low lows. Whatever frequency they are on, they bring you right with them. If they are in a great mood, you will likely match their energy. However, if they are in a bad mood, they will drag you right down with them. They have some great qualities, but with those, come the bad. If you are a Cancer, I suggest you make the effort be more mindful of some of your less favorable traits. I have provided you with some traits that shouldn't be considered a big deal, however, these traits can affect your relationships with others without you even realizing it.

Sensitive: The Cancer is probably the most sensitive sign of them all. Even the littlest thing can upset a Cancer. The worst thing is, they *are* aware of how sensitive they are (and critical of themselves for it), so they usually do not tell you when you've upset them.

As a Cancer, you take things very personally. Whether it be something that someone said, or something they didn't say. If you are a Cancer, it is important to avoid taking everything personally in life. People in this world are not out to hurt you, and I think you need to understand that a little better. If you find yourself easily triggered, it's important you open up to loved ones so that they can avoid hurting you in the future.

Emotional: The Cancer is a water sign, therefore, you can count on them to take you on an emotional roller coaster ride. They tend to feel everything on a much deeper level. If they are happy, they are on top of the world! When they are sad, they get into a dark, depressive state. When they are angry, all hell breaks loose, and you see a whole other side of the Cancer. If you are a Cancer, it will be very helpful to you if you make the effort to react using logic and reason, rather than your heart. When you live through logic, you will find that your emotions are stable, and easier to manage.

Insecure: The insecurity in the Cancer is rooted in their sensitivity and emotions. If you work on these two traits, you will notice that you are more secure with yourself. The Cancer's insecurities can affect their relationships in many ways. They are constantly seeking validation and reassurance from others due to their lack of confidence. An insecure Cancer is typically an unevolved Cancer. They have not reached their full potential, due to the fact that their insecurities are holding them back in many ways.

Zodiac Signs Unlocked: The Ugly

The toxic trait you need to be aware of: Being manipulative

How this affects my...

Relationships: Once people see the manipulative side of you, it is very hard to go back. It will push people away.

Productivity: Instead of finding solutions, you usually manipulate your way through situations or relationships. This always has an expiry date and will become toxic very fast.

Mental state: Once everything has blown over, and the damage is done, you often live with regret or guilt. This might take you a while to get over, and holding on to this will affect your thoughts and emotions.

Digging Deeper...

Toxic trait: Being manipulative

The Cancer can be one of the most manipulative signs in the zodiac. As a Cancer, you go above and beyond for your loved ones. You have a habit of doing too much for people who don't always deserve it. Because of this, you are taken advantage of quite often.

You are very kind, and even when you realize you are being mistreated; you tend to hold it in. The problem is that you are building up resentment and anger toward others since you are not communicating this. Eventually, you snap, and it isn't pretty. You can get very malicious and emotional, and you will begin to go out of your way to hurt those who have mistreated you, instead of just having a conversation. You want to make them feel what they've made *you* feel, and this gets extremely manipulative. You know all the buttons to push, which could include sensitive topics, insecurities, or low blows. What you fail to realize, Cancer, is that things cannot be left unsaid.

If it doesn't get to this point, a Cancer will typically use digs to remind people in their lives of all they have done for them. They will use this against them in arguments as a manipulation tactic. It is important that as a Cancer, you do things wholeheartedly and without expectations. If someone isn't reciprocating, communicate your feelings before it gets out of hand. People are not mind readers.

Where Do I Begin?

I will tell you the same thing that I have told every single zodiac sign. Begin with the end in mind. Where do you see yourself at end of this mindfulness journey? Don't take the word "end" too seriously; this is a lifelong journey. It is important to understand where you see yourself after you have done all the crucial healing and inner work. That will keep you in alignment with your purpose. To understand your purpose, ask yourself the following three questions. These have all been customized to your moon sign. You can apply them to your sun sign as well.

1. How can I feel comfortable enough to open up to others about how I am feeling?

2. Where is the malicious side of me coming from, and how can I heal this?

3. How can I learn to only seek validation from myself?

CHAPTER 5

The Leo

July 23-August 22

Ruling planet: Sun ☉ **Element:** Fire △ **Symbol:** The Lion ♌
Quality: Fixed **Opposite sign:** Aquarius

Self-Awareness

As a Leo, you might think that you barely have any flaws (it's OK, sometimes I wish I had the confidence of a Leo!). I'm sure that you are aware of the fact that you are not perfect, but you may have a hard time figuring out what exactly your flaws are. Or maybe, you *are* aware of your flaws, but you expect everyone else to adjust to them and "get used to it," because that's who you are.

Well I'm here to tell you that it's not OK to just accept certain behaviors. Of course, there are certain aspects of our personalities that are embedded in us, but there are many behaviors and thought patterns that we are able to relearn with enough inner work. Break the cycle of toxic behaviors and make the choice to change. Deep down, I know you have an idea as to what traits of yours can be considered toxic. Get to the root of them, and figure out what's next.

Step 1: Ask the people you love what your best and worst qualities are

A great way for you to become more self-aware would be to ask your friends and family to tell you what some of your best and worst personality traits are. I know it won't be easy for you to sit down and read a list of all the shitty things about your personality. No one wants to do that. That's why you're asking for the good *and* the bad. For every terrible trait, there is an amazing one to go right along with it. You can feed your ego, but also learn what you may need to work on! Just remember, you asked for it.

This isn't your best friend who is jealously trying to attack you, and this isn't your mother out to get you. This is for your benefit, so be open-minded and ready to receive! This step is important to you as a Leo, simply because you value the opinions of others. You care what people think about you—especially the people you love. Use this to your advantage.

Step 2: Decide whether or not you agree with the traits on the list

Narrow down your list and truly decide what you resonate with. It's OK to disagree, but make sure you are being honest with yourself. If four people mention that you are self-centered, then you probably are. If you disagree with certain points, spend some extra time analyzing these parts of yourself. You could possess certain traits that you have never even realized before! TRUST ME. It took me twenty-four years to realize I was selfish. It's never too late. You just have to be honest with yourself.

Step 3: Tell your loved ones about your mindfulness journey

Tell everyone around you about the inner work you are doing! Hold yourself accountable to this process. As a Leo, you are a hard worker. You can't stand the thought of failing. Even worse, you can't stand the idea of others seeing you fail.

If you tell loved ones about your mindfulness journey, they will become aware of your progress! This means that you will be extremely aware of your behaviors because that last thing you want is *Becky* telling you that you are going back to your old ways. This is a tricky step though. It is easy to let your ego get in the way and become the motivating force behind the inner work. Make sure that the desire to change is rooted in all the right reasons. Don't do it for *Becky,* do it for YOU.

Step 4: Write down all your accomplishments!

Every time you recognize progress, write it down! If you are working on being less selfish, write down any moment in which you realize you are practicing generosity. Keep a list of all the moments you see progress and read it at the end of each week! Once you see results, this will motivate you to work harder!

You are in constant competition with yourself, so this will push you to become an even better you! The more you read it, the more you will realize just how far you've come. This is very important! This will keep you on track, and remind you why you began this self-improvement journey in the first place. I believe in you!

Zodiac Signs Unlocked: The Good

The Leo is one of those signs that everyone loves to hate. They get a lot of attention, sometimes good, and sometimes bad. Here's the thing about the Leo—if they are in your social circle, they are the absolute best person to be around! They are the life of the party, and they will make sure everyone is taken care of.

I remember in college; I had a close friend who was a Leo. She was always the one at parties making sure everyone had a drink in hand, and wouldn't let anyone stand alone! She'd make sure that everyone was socializing and having a good time even though she wasn't the host! She enjoyed taking care of others.

Leos often get a bad rep because most people are familiar with their less favorable traits. The Leo has many stereotypes surrounding them. They are such a well-known sign that people who aren't even into astrology will say "I knew you were a Leo!" because their personality is just that vibrant. They are caring and loyal. They will show you parts of yourself that you didn't know you even had! The typical Leo (sun, moon, or rising) may display some of the following traits:

- ⊙ **Sun:** Energetic, extroverted, kind, hilarious, talkative, friendly, attractive

- ☽ **Moon:** Kind, sympathetic, responsible, loving, accepting

- ↑ **Rising:** Confident, loud, bubbly, funny, outgoing, brave

The Evolved Leo

If you're a Leo, chances are, people know who you are before you introduce yourself. Whether they know of you, or they know your name and story, either way, they're familiar with you. You grasp the attention of the room, sometimes without even trying.

Leos have a bad reputation for being self-centered, and egotistical. Yes, this applies to many Leos, however, these are the unevolved Leos. An evolved Leo is confident, not cocky. They are attention grabbers, not attention seekers. They radiate confidence, and it's hard not to be pulled in by the magnetic force of a self-assured Leo.

Leos are much more than this though. They are actually very sweet and compassionate. They will do anything for their loved ones, especially their significant others. A Leo that is evolved is someone who goes out of their way to help and teach others. They want to succeed in life, and only want the same for others. No one matches the drive of a Leo. Leos are the hardest workers you will come across. Nothing is getting in the way of what they desire out of life. I mean it. They set goals, and they meet them. If they are ever in a position that could be considered "failure," it only pushes them to work harder. If you do not resonate with this and you are a Leo, don't give up. This is who you are meant to be. You have all the potential to become this confident, hardworking individual. It's in there somewhere, you just have to do the inner work.

Zodiac Signs Unlocked: The Bad

The Leo is one of those signs that people love to hate, but they don't care. Any type of attention is good attention. If you didn't know this already, Leos are known for their attention-seeking personality. They must have all eyes on them, and they are constantly brainstorming new ways to impress others. Although this sounds harmless, it can come off very negatively to certain personality types. If you are a Leo, I suggest you make the effort be more mindful of some of your less favorable traits. I have provided you with some traits that shouldn't be considered a big deal. However, these traits can affect your relationships with others without you even realizing it.

Arrogant: The Leo can come off as extremely arrogant without even realizing it. They love to talk about themselves, even if it means talking over someone else. They have a bad habit of trying to outshine others, but many times, they don't even realize they're doing it. They can't help but grasp the attention of others. A Leo is the type to out-dress the bride on her wedding day. If you are a Leo, I suggest taking a moment out of the spotlight every now and then. Let others have their moment.

Patronizing: Leos are quite knowledgeable in many areas. They have a tendency to use their knowledge to belittle others. They like to be in a position of power, and they feel as though "power" is in knowing. They can be very patronizing, especially if you get on their bad side. Common phrases for a Leo include: "I told you so" and "I already knew that." They are very quick to point out when someone is wrong, or knows less than them, however, they will never admit it if they are that person. In their eyes, they know everything. At least, that's what they want you to think.

Inability to compromise: Leos have a hard time compromising with others. They are very self-involved; therefore, they constantly believe that their way is always the best way to get something done. They can be quite stubborn in their ways. Therefore they rarely try to find a happy medium with others. If they do come to a compromise, they manipulate the situation to make it seem as if it were their idea, and it can get quite frustrating. If you are a Leo, try your hardest to be mindful in these times, as it can get quite old, fast.

Zodiac Signs Unlocked: The Ugly

The toxic trait you need to be aware of: Self-centeredness

How this affects my...

Relationships: People feel neglected by you because you are too focused on yourself.

Productivity: When you are too focused on your self-image, you miss the bigger picture.

Mental state: Constantly trying to impress people will bring you further from who you truly are.

Digging Deeper...

Toxic trait: Self-centeredness

The Leo is a very confident sign, but at times, it can get out of hand. Because of their arrogance, they have a sense of entitlement. They can be extremely self-centered, and act as though the world revolves around them. I mean their ruling planet is the sun, so can you blame them?

Unevolved Leos are usually unaware that they are self-centered, and this is the problem. They don't realize that because they are so focused on their own lives, they are neglecting their loved ones. If someone close to them is going through something, it is very likely that they will fail to realize until they are told. They can be quite distant in relationships because of this.

If you are a Leo, it is extremely important that you are self-aware enough to realize when you are neglecting basic emotional needs in a relationship. If you realize that your friends stopped opening up to you, it could be because every time they did, you changed the topic to your own personal issues. If people stopped inviting you out, it might be because you demanded too much attention. Not all Leos are like this, but it is important to know if you fall into this category of Leos because if so, you are probably very difficult to be around.

Where Do I Begin?

I will tell you the same thing that I have told every single zodiac sign. Begin with the end in mind. Where do you see yourself at end of this mindfulness journey? Don't take the word "end" too seriously; this is a lifelong journey. It is important to understand where you see yourself after you have done all the crucial healing and inner work. That will keep you in alignment with your purpose. To understand your purpose, ask yourself the following three questions. These have all been customized to your moon sign. You can apply them to your sun sign as well.

1. How can I humble myself?

2. Why do I feel the need to constantly impress others?

3. What deeply rooted issues do I need to heal so that I can feel confident without any validation from others?

CHAPTER 6

The Virgo

August 23–September 22

Ruling planet: Mercury ☿ **Element:** Earth ▽ **Symbol:** The Virgin ♍
Quality: Mutable **Opposite sign:** Pisces

Self-Awareness

Oh, Virgo... Before I even begin, I just want to tell you: Stop being so hard on yourself! Seriously. You are your own biggest critic. If there is one Zodiac sign that is already self-aware, it's the Virgo. You spend so much time analyzing yourself and the world around you; it's rare that I meet a Virgo that is not self-aware. Those ones are the unevolved Virgos.

An unevolved Virgo is usually very content with who they are, and live in their own little bubble. The problem with the unevolved Virgo, however, is that they constantly find themselves in bad cycles. Whether the cycle is constantly getting yourself in relationships that don't work out, always ending up in jobs you hate, losing friends regularly...you name it! If you find yourself in these toxic patterns, and have no idea why—I'll tell you! YOU may be the problem. That's OK though. We've all been there. I know I have (and it took me a long time to see it, especially with my moon in Virgo). Break the cycle and change your life! It all starts with *you*.

Step 1: Get in nature and do some deep self-reflection

As an earth sign, you do a lot of your best thinking in nature. Ditch the music, phone, and any other distractions. You need this time to be alone in your thoughts. Write down a list of all the recurring issues that you come across in life that you never really get clarity on. Bring this list with you, and go outside. I suggest a walk through a forest, a meadow, a hill, or maybe even by a body of water. Once you've found a sacred space, go over each point on this list individually and ask yourself the following questions:

1. What was my role in this situation?

2. What do all these situations have in common?

3. Am I the problem? Why or why not?

4. How can I avoid this next time?

Step 2: Find a pattern

Once you've found a pattern in all these situations, get to the root of it. For example, if you realize that the reason you lost your job, best friend, and significant other is because you didn't put enough effort, figure out why! When did this begin? Childhood? How else has this lack of effort affected your life and relationships? Why are you this way? Keep asking yourself questions until you get to the bottom of it.

Step 3: Meditate

I know you have a lot of thoughts. Your mind is constantly running. Silence your thoughts for a moment, and declutter your brain. Meditate. This will allow you to think clearly, which will make this self-reflection much more meaningful. There will be more tips on meditation later on in the book, but I will suggest the best method for you as a Virgo right here. Guided meditation! As a Virgo, your mind is louder than the average person. Meditation can be quite difficult for you because you find silencing your thoughts nearly impossible. If you try out a guided mediation, you are following the sound of someone's voice, therefore focusing on them, rather than telling your brain to shut up. This will go a long way. Trust me!

Step 4: Journal

After meditation, take the time to journal. This is when your mind is clearest, and you will find that it is easier to articulate your thoughts in this state. Write down what you are thinking and feeling in that moment. Write down what made you sad, happy, angry, or grateful that day. Re-read your entries every now and then and find patterns in your thought processes. When you do this, you are getting to know yourself better and better. This will make it much easier for you to figure out who you truly are as an individual. Again, try not to be so critical of yourself. I know you are a perfectionist and want to become your best self over night. I only wish it were that easy. You are already amazing! You got this, Virgo!

Zodiac Signs Unlocked: The Good

I'm going to tell you something that you probably already know: Virgos are the smartest sign of the zodiac. It has a lot to do with the fact that you love to learn. You immerse yourself in knowledge, whether it be books, articles, or hours of YouTube videos. I consider a Virgo who is very close to me a walking encyclopedia. No matter what I ask, he seems to have all the answers. If he doesn't, he will make sure to do his research and come back to me with them. It is all this knowledge that gives the Virgo so much confidence! You are bright, yet humble (some of you). You carry yourself in a way in which people know they can't mess with you. You are selfless when it comes to people that you love, and it takes a lot for you to get upset or angry. Your positive aura is nearly untouchable. The typical Virgo (sun, moon, or rising) may display some of the following traits:

Sun: Practical, caring, considerate, charming, wise, empathetic, sensible, realistic, dependable

Moon: Loving, selfless, affectionate, helpful, kind-hearted, gentle, dedicated, loyal, sensitive, emotional

Rising: Charismatic, analytical, witty, humane, helpful, sincere, clever

The Evolved Virgo

I'm just going to come right out and say it…Virgo is my favorite sign. Well, the evolved Virgo that is. An unevolved Virgo can be one of the most toxic signs, but we'll get there in a moment. The evolved Virgo is someone you don't want to let go of. They are practical, dependable and kind. They are some of the most selfless people you will ever meet. If you ever need anything from them, you don't have to ask twice. In fact, you probably won't even have to ask. They are always one step ahead of you, especially if you are romantically involved with one. Trust me, I've been there. The Virgo is one of the most analytical signs I have ever met. You can't slide anything past them. Don't even try to lie to them! They will be onto you in a second.

They are hardworking, intelligent, and creative. Almost every Virgo I've ever met is in some sort of creative industry. They have a hard time living by societal norms, so they work hard at what they are passionate about. A Virgo that is evolved is self-aware enough to know what they want out of life. Their passion and drive will make it happen, and they will bring people along with them. If they eat, everybody eats. If you do not resonate with the traits of an evolved Virgo, you got some work to do. That's

OK! Once you become the best version of yourself, you will be untouchable. Your confidence will land you opportunities you once dreamed of, but your humbleness will keep you grounded.

Zodiac Signs Unlocked: The Bad

The Virgo is one of those signs that everyone gets along with, and they work very hard to make sure of this. Virgos have a habit of amplifying their personality to get in the good graces of others. Oftentimes, they have a hidden agenda with everyone they meet. They are kind and loving people; however, they can be very sneaky and manipulative at times. They are some of the smartest people you will ever meet. Be very careful when dealing with an unevolved Virgo. If you are an unevolved Virgo, I suggest you make the effort be more mindful of some of your less favorable traits. I have provided you with some traits that shouldn't be considered a big deal, however, these traits can affect your relationships with others without you even realizing it.

All-talk, no action: Virgos have a tendency to be very vocal about the things they desire. They speak too soon, before putting a plan into action. A Virgo is the type of person that will talk about starting a business, take the first two steps to start it, then neglect the whole project entirely and never mention it again. They will do this again months later, and it ends up being a repeated cycle.

They don't do this intentionally; they just get bored easily. This trait causes the Virgo to have a reputation for making empty promises as well. They often express all the things they want to do for you, but never follow through. Their heart is in the right place, they just never actually get around to putting a plan into action. The problem is, they think they have time.

Untidy: The Virgos are known to be very organized so this might come as a shock to you, but the Virgo can actually be very untidy. Usually in their work office space, you will find an organized chaos. They usually have a system in place, and know where everything is, however, from the outside looking in, it looks like a straight-up mess. Don't try cleaning their space. They love their organized mess.

Stubborn: I feel as though many people don't talk about it, but Virgo is one of the most stubborn signs you will come across. They are extremely hardheaded, and it is very difficult to change their opinion on something. Don't even try debating with one! They could go on for days. Sometimes they forget what they are even arguing about. They just love to prove a point and hear the words "You're right."

Zodiac Signs Unlocked: The Ugly

The toxic trait you need to be aware of: Sneaky

How this affects my...

Relationships: Your sneaky behavior can cause you to lie or cheat. This is often unforgiveable, and you will lose a lot of people because of this.

Productivity: You will try to take the easy way out at times, and although it may feel productive, you are not truly learning anything. You are stunting your own growth.

Mental state: As an emotional sign, you will have a lot of guilt in you. This will not be easy for you to deal with, and can lead to a lot of anxiety or depression (depending on the circumstances).

Digging Deeper....

Toxic trait: Sneaky

The Virgo is known to be extremely sneaky at times. They are the type of sign that will steal your boyfriend/girlfriend with no remorse. They are very smart people. They use their knowledge to go after what they want, even if it's not in the most ethical ways.

As a Virgo, you might find yourself in many situations that can be easily fixed with a lie. This is never the answer! Although small lies don't hurt every now and then, the Virgo is one of those signs that will tell a huge lie to cover up something that could potentially hurt their loved ones. A lie hurts more than the truth, and the trust always comes out. Trust me.

Virgos sneaky-ness comes out in many different types of situations, but the root of the issue is usually that they are protecting someone's feelings. As Virgo, it is important that you understand that this does not make it okay at all. Deal with your baggage early on, or it will come back to bite you in the ass. The backlash will be much uglier than it could've been. It makes more sense to face it head-on, and get it over with.

Where Do I Begin?

I will tell you the same thing that I have told every single zodiac sign. Begin with the end in mind. Where do you see yourself at end of this mindfulness journey? Don't take the word "end" too seriously; this is a lifelong journey. It is important to understand where you see yourself after you have done all the crucial healing and inner work. That will keep you in alignment with your purpose. To understand your purpose, ask yourself the following three questions. These have all been customized to your moon sign. You can apply it to your sun sign as well.

1. What causes me to be so defensive?

2. How can I learn to put less pressure on myself and others?

3. What is causing me to be dishonest with my loved ones?

CHAPTER 7

THE LIBRA

September 23-October 23

Ruling planet: Venus ♀ **Element:** Air △ **Symbol:** The Scales ♎
Quality: Cardinal **Opposite sign:** Aries

Self-Awareness

As a Libra, you have probably already thought about your mindfulness journey. You probably have an idea as to what you want to work on, and you've made a choice to improve yourself. Some of you may not resonate with this, but I'm guessing you're waiting for the right time. You think you'll wake up one day and decide you're ready to begin your self-improvement process. You're constantly putting mental roadblocks on this process, but this is just prolonging it further. There is always time. You are just not making it a priority. Life is all about balance, isn't it? Find a way to add inner work into your daily routine, and you will find a way to create that balance. There is never going to be a "right time," because it's always the right time. Put yourself first!

Step 1: Make the decision to work on yourself and stick to it!

Libras have a hard time making decisions; we know this. Sit down and decide that working on mindfulness is a priority. Make that decision to add it to your daily routine. Say it out loud, write it down, and affirm it. Program your brain into recognizing that working on yourself is just as important as finishing up that college essay, or getting your daily hour in the gym! Add it to your calendar, put time aside to journal or meditate, and make it just as important as some of your other daily tasks. Once you make the decision to acknowledge the importance of this self-love journey, it will be easier for you to want to put in the work. It might take a few weeks to truly make it a habit, but be patient with yourself. Eventually, it will become second nature.

Step 2: Talk to your loved ones

Sometimes, you just need to let it out. Although journaling will be great for you, another method of self-reflection is talking to your friends about what you are feeling and thinking. Vent to the people you trust about what you're going through, and seek out advice. You are someone who is extremely open-minded, and maybe you just need that second opinion for something to truly click in your brain. You may feel like a victim in a situation, but after speaking to someone you trust, you could discover that you are actually in the wrong. Be very selective with whom you speak. Make sure you are only seeking out the opinions of those are wise and unbiased.

Step 3: Don't overwhelm yourself

As you begin this mindfulness journey, you might realize that you have fifty different traits you want to work on and improve. Set goals and be realistic. If you realized that you are too sensitive, work on that. Once you have done enough inner work and feel as though your sensitivity is at a healthy level, then work on your next trait. Don't overwhelm yourself and try to improve everything in a month. You will be discouraged and feel as though you've failed. It might help you write make a checklist of all the things you want to improve. Check off each box (even if you only check one off a month!) and watch your list get smaller and smaller.

Step 4: Ask loved ones about your progress

As I mentioned, you value the opinions of others. This isn't a bad thing. Every now and then, it might be very productive of you to ask others about your progress. If you feel as though you are improving, or even if you're unsure, ask a friend. Ask if they've noticed changed behaviors, or if you have gotten better at whatever it is that you are working on. If they are a real friend, they will be honest with you! If they haven't noticed improvement, work harder! If they have, pat yourself on the back and keep going. You're becoming better and better every day. Once day you will see it, and so will they! Everything is going to be OK.

Zodiac Signs Unlocked: The Good

The Libra is the most neutral, unproblematic person you will ever come across. I've never encountered a Libra that I didn't like. Seriously. You guys are just so easy going. I understand not being indifferent toward a Libra you may have met, but disliking one is very out of the ordinary. Libras are friendly and open. They are easy to get into deep conversations with. In fact, if you are a Libra, you probably find yourself having long conversations with strangers very often.

My best friend Monika is a Libra, and she is constantly getting into deep conversations with people she has known for minutes! People love to tell her all about their life, and somehow, she makes them comfortable enough to open up and share extremely personal details! If you are a Libra, I bet the strangers even open up to you, and you leave the conversation wondering why the hell they just told you their life story. It's totally normal for you guys. Embrace it. It makes life a lot more interesting, trust me. If you are a Libra, you might have a hard time trying to figure out who you are. Don't worry, I'm here to help. The typical Libra (sun, moon, or rising) may display some of the following traits:

- **Sun:** Witty, bubbly, open, friendly, sweet, logical, fair, courteous, wise

- **Moon:** Balanced, loving, honest, loyal, communicative, romantic

↑ **Rising:** Charming, graceful, cooperative, opinionated, leader

The Evolved Libra

The evolved Libra is graceful and kind. Many Libras have the tendency to be rather narcissistic (to be discussed later), but the evolved version of this zodiac sign is the complete opposite. They are selfless and loving. They care deeply for others. They always strive for harmonious relationships, and will do whatever they can to maintain that balance. They are practical, and very good at communicating. It is rare to find a Libra in conflict.

An unevolved Libra avoids conflict and confrontation, but an evolved Libra rarely faces it. They are able to mediate a situation before it becomes a massive conflict. They do this by reason, viewing everything from a logical perspective before reacting. This will go a long way. The overthinking Libra often has a hard time dealing with complicated situations; however, once you have evolved, everything will change. Even something as simple as making a decision will be much easier for you. With self-awareness, you barely have any space in your mind to question anything. You know what you want, or what you don't want. Life is much easier. You spend less time making decisions. This may not sound like a big deal, but when it comes to big life changes, making a decision is all that matters. An evolved Libra is able to have peace of mind, knowing that they are self-assured and confident in everything they do.

Zodiac Signs Unlocked: The Bad

In my opinion, the Libra can also be one of the most annoying zodiac signs. Sorry, I had to say it. Sometimes, they can be so wonderful and unproblematic, other times I have to sit and wonder how they get by in life. The Libra is one of the most easy-going, yet difficult signs you will come across. They are very difficult to please at times, and aren't shy to admit it. If you are an unevolved Libra, I suggest you make the effort to be more mindful of some of your less favorable traits. I have provided you with some traits that shouldn't be considered a big deal, however, these traits can affect your relationships with others without you even realizing it.

Fearful: The Libra is one of those signs who is scared of the entire world. Sometimes, they attempt to put up a façade, as if nothing fazes them, but when push comes to shove, they are wimps. They usually have many fears, and no desire to work through them. They accept them as they are, and because of this, many Libras miss out on the best parts of life. If you are a Libra, make an effort to step outside your comfort zone as often as possible and explore what life has to offer.

Indecisive: The Libra is known for being indecisive, and it can be very frustrating. They constantly weigh over their options, and overthink possible outcomes much more than they should. Their inability to make a decision comes from fear. Fear that they are making the wrong choice. Sometimes, you just have to live and learn. Libras would rather get things right the first time than to live and learn. What Libras don't tend to realize, is that having too many options can actually lead to more stress and anxiety. They spend so much time weighing all their options and possible outcomes, they end up stressing themselves out to the point that they rarely enjoy it.

Whiners/complainers: I have never in my life met a sign that loves to complain as much as the Libra. The Libra has a hard time accepting when things are not going the way they hoped, and they are not shy about it! They spend a lot of their time whining and complaining. I don't think they realize the effect it has on others. They get into a negative mindset, and like to stay there and dwell for a while. If you are a Libra, become very aware of this. It may sound harmless, but negative talk can really bring yourself and others down. Another one of my Libra friends can be extremely pessimistic. He spends a lot of his time putting himself down. If you find yourself doing that, try approaching life with "glass half-full" mentality and see how your life changes.

Zodiac Signs Unlocked: The Ugly

The toxic trait you need to be aware of: Dependency

How this affects my...

Relationships: Your partners might deem you as clingy or needy because of your dependency.

Productivity: You wait for others to be of assistance before getting something done on your own. When you depend on others, you are working on their time.

Mental State: You stay in your comfort zone, depending on others. This can lead to a lot of disappointment.

Digging Deeper...

Toxic trait: Dependency

The Libra is known to be one of the most dependent signs out of the zodiac. They are the type of people who can't run an errand without calling five people to see if one of them can accompany them first. The problem is, when a Libra is very close to someone, the people around him or her tend to get frustrated with them because of their lack of independence. Libras tend to rely on the people very close to them, for even the smallest things. Often, they can allow themselves to be stagnant in life because they are too dependent. They won't take initiative because they are waiting on someone else. This trait can cause codependency in romantic relationships, which is very unhealthy.

If you are a Libra, be very mindful of this trait. Make sure that you are self-sufficient and whole before entering a romantic partnership. It is easy for you to become reliant on another person, but this can be prevented. The last thing you want is to get into a partnership in which you feel as though you can not walk away because your life relies heavily on the other person. Practice solitude, and being okay with being alone. People aren't always going to be there. Do not wait for them. Make things happen for yourself, by yourself.

Where Do I Begin?

I will tell you the same thing that I have told every single zodiac sign. Begin with the end in mind. Where do you see yourself at end of this mindfulness journey? Don't take the word "end" too seriously; this is a lifelong journey. It is important to understand where you see yourself after you have done all the crucial healing and inner work. That will keep you in alignment with your purpose. To understand your purpose, ask yourself the following three questions. These have all been customized to your moon sign. You can apply it to your sun sign as well.

1. How can I learn to feel comfortable with confrontation when necessary?

2. Why do I allow myself to be dependent on others, and how can I learn to trust myself?

3. Why do I feel fear so often? What is causing this?

CHAPTER 8

THE SCORPIO

October 24-November 21

Ruling planet: Pluto/Mars ♀ / ♂ **Element:** Water ▽
Symbol: The Scorpion ♏ **Quality:** Fixed **Opposite sign:** Taurus

Self-Awareness

Oh, dear Scorpio. You are a complex, misunderstood sign. You probably feel as though you are in this alone. You definitely aren't, but I know better than to tell you to talk to a friend. You probably want to go through this self-awareness journey all on your own, but that's more than OK! As long as you want to begin this journey, that's all that matters. Because the truth is, you are all that you need. Seriously. We came into this world alone, and we will die alone. As long as you are there for yourself, that is what really matters.

Step 1: Isolation and expression

You do your best thinking alone. I guess we all do, but no one loves their solitude as much as a Scorpio (Aquarius does come pretty close though). Find a place where you will be uninterrupted, and do some deep self-reflection. You are a very expressive person, so use this time to express yourself. Whatever it is that fuels you, do that. It could be writing poetry, cooking, making videos, photography, or painting. Whatever it is, do it! Clear that space in your mind. Express yourself.

Step 2: Reflect on your emotions

As a water sign, you are a very emotional being. Once you have released some emotions by expressing yourself through your creative outlet, your mind should be a little more at peace. This state of mind is probably best for self-refection. Write down how you are feeling. If you have a hard time doing that, look up journaling prompts online, or ask yourself the questions given at the beginning of this chapter. If you are feeling a negative emotion, figure out what triggered it and why. If you are feeling positive, question what made you happy and do more of that!

Step 3: Be more present

As a Scorpio, you can be quite absent. Oftentimes, you dissociate from reality and this is what can cause you to overreact or show a lack of interest in things or people that may actually be very important to you. This can affect your happiness, even if you don't realize it. If you practice being more present, you will become much more aware. You will be more aware of your surroundings, and even of yourself. This will make this process so much easier for you! A way that you can practice being present is by taking five long, deep breaths. Re-center yourself, and bring yourself back into the present moment. I know it sounds simple, but it can go a long way.

Step 4: Practice vulnerability

I know this one is probably really difficult for you. As a Scorpio, you like to maintain this appearance of always having it together. It's OK not to be OK, and I think it's time you accept that. When you practice vulnerability, you are staying true to yourself. You will find it easier to accept yourself. Once you find this acceptance within yourself, this journey to self-awareness will become less painful. Allow yourself to be vulnerable. Not just with yourself, but with others. You are not an emotionless robot. You're human. Not only are you human, you are a water sign. This heartless act isn't fooling anyone, so embrace it. You're amazing!

Zodiac Signs Unlocked: The Good

The Scorpio is definitely the most mysterious out of all the zodiac signs. It's very likely that you are reading this chapter, not because you are a Scorpio, but because you are trying to pick apart the mind of a Scorpio that won't let you in. To the actual

Scorpios that are reading this: lighten up. I understand you don't want to let just anyone in, but people care more about you than you think.

Scorpios are one of the most loved zodiac signs. Oddly enough, they are also the most hated. This is mostly because once you cross a Scorpio, you pretty much have a death wish. But only *if* you cross them. If you want to get to know this sign better, you've come to the right place. I was best friends with a Scorpio for years, and she was one of the most loving and loyal people I knew. However, once there was a disconnect in our friendship, she started to distance herself emotionally, it seemed. It was only when the friendship slowly started to fade that her loyalty ran out. I didn't understand it at the time, but now I know why. Scorpios are only loyal to a fault. The typical Scorpio (sun, moon, or rising) may display some of the following traits:

- **Sun:** Interesting, bubbly, open, friendly, scandalous, protective, compassionate

- **Moon:** Emotional, sensual, intense, loving, sensitive, magnetic, understanding, open

- **Rising:** Private, invigorating, trustworthy, mysterious, loyal

The Evolved Scorpio

Being a Scorpio, your life is probably extremely intense. Your friendships are intense. Your thoughts are intense. Your environment is intense. It's almost like you enjoy living in chaos. Somehow you manage.

The evolved Scorpio can balance everything important to them in life. You are very humble, and never forget who you are, or where you came from. You love extremely hard and without limits. You tear down the wall that the unevolved Scorpio built up, and you allow yourself to be vulnerable with those who deserve to have access to this side of you. You are extremely caring, and sensitive to others. You want the best for those around you, but sometimes you may have a hard time showing it.

The evolved Scorpio has usually done some inner work to control their emotions. You take things less personally, and you are less reactive to those who mistreat you. You are able to step outside of your emotions, and look at a situation from a mature and logical perspective. You have learned to think with your head, and not your heart. You care deeply for your loved ones, and would do anything for them. If there is one sign that I can guarantee loyalty from, it's the Scorpio. But only if you deserve it.

Zodiac Signs Unlocked: The Bad

Moody: The Scorpio is one of those signs that you never really know which version of them you are going to get. They can be some of the most happy and loveable people, but then they can get into a mood. When they get moody, their entire personality changes. Usually, it comes out of nowhere. It could be something as simple as them getting a text they don't like, or someone saying the wrong thing, that will put them into a mood. They usually don't communicate either. Their aura just changes, and no one knows why. Dear Scorpios, it's OK to be affected. It's OK to be in a bad mood. What is not OK is leaving your loved ones in the dark all the time. If someone bothers you, say so; that way they can correct their behavior. Give people a chance.

Jealous: The Scorpio has an issue with jealousy. They have a hard time controlling it. The jealousy comes from the fact that they make assumptions, but don't ask enough questions. They don't like to express their jealousy. Therefore, whatever is making them jealous is something they usually have to deal with in their own mind. They don't seek reassurance because their ego will not allow them to admit they are jealous to their loved one. They feel jealousy in every relationship, whether it is a family member, friend, romantic partner, or even work relationships! If you are a Scorpio, asking questions and getting that reassurance is worth it for your peace of mind. Drop the ego, and do what you need to do to feel better.

Secretive: The Scorpio has a tendency to be extremely secretive for absolutely no reason at all. They like to keep their life extremely private. This is something that they struggle with in relationships. They want to keep too much of their life private, and this can seriously affect the other person. Even if they aren't doing anything bad, they still want to hide certain parts of their life.

For example, I remember while I was friends with the same Scorpio I just mentioned, she would go out of her way to hide things from me for no apparent reason. I'd ask her what her plans were on any given evening and she'd say, "I'm going out."

So I'd ask where and she'd say, "Out." If I even dared ask a third time, she'd usually respond by saying, "somewhere," with a lot of attitude. I never really understood why, but now I know that it's just a Scorpio thing to feel entitled to privacy at all times. Even with small, insignificant details. They are very protective of themselves, and don't allow many people to get too close for fear of being hurt. As a Scorpio, be mindful of the things you want to keep private, especially when it comes to romantic relationships. Having privacy is OK, but if certain hidden parts of your life make your partner uncomfortable, decide if it's really worth it to hold onto that privacy.

Zodiac Signs Unlocked: The Ugly

The toxic trait you need to be aware of: Self-destructive

How this affects my...

Relationships: You push away people who are trying to love and be there for you.

Productivity: You are so focused on people and things that add no value to your life, that you do not have time to be productive.

Mental state: You are not prioritizing yourself; therefore, this will cause an eventual downfall. As a water sign, the emotions that follow the downfall will affect you deeply.

Digging Deeper...

Toxic trait: Self-destructive

The Scorpio is a sign that has a hard time accepting when things are going well. In their mind, everything is too good to be true. They are a very emotional sign, and do not deal with disappointment well. It is because of this that Scorpios have a habit of self-sabotaging. They set themselves up for disappointment so that they don't have their hopes up for something that may not go their way.

For example, if they are in a job interview that they realize is not going well, it is likely that they will mentally check out of the conversation so that they can leave the interaction knowing that they didn't get the job, rather than giving it a full chance and risking rejection. The unevolved Scorpio can be self-destructive in many different parts of their life. They give up very easily, so they can always be prepared for the outcome, whether it be good or bad. If you are an unevolved Scorpio, you could be missing out on many great opportunities. Try to have a more optimistic view on life. It will take you very far. Remember, you miss 100 percent of the shots you don't take. (I know that quote is super cheesy, but you're a water sign so I know you'll appreciate it.)

Where Do I Begin?

I will tell you the same thing that I have told every single zodiac sign. Begin with the end in mind. Where do you see yourself at end of this mindfulness journey? Don't take the word "end" too seriously; this is a lifelong journey. It is important to understand where you see yourself after you have done all the crucial healing and inner work. That will keep you in alignment with your purpose. To understand your purpose, ask yourself the following three questions. These have all been customized to your moon sign. You can apply it to your sun sign as well.

1. Why do I keep my life so private from people that I trust?

2. What causes me to self-destruct when things are going my way?

3. How can I learn to open up to others?

CHAPTER 9

THE SAGITTARIUS

November 22-December 21

Ruling planet: Jupiter ♃ Element: Fire △ Symbol: The Archer ↗
Quality: Mutable Opposite sign: Gemini

Self-Awareness

One of my favorite things about the Sagittarius is that you tend to take feedback well. Whether it is good or bad. You are not one of those zodiac signs that gets extremely defensive, and this will be very beneficial to you during this process. You already made the decision to purchase this book, which means you are ready to make a change. You have so much potential, and it all starts with self-awareness. These steps below can kick start your journey.

Step 1: Get to know your inner child

The people and world around you have impacted who you are today. Who were you before your environment tainted your reality? Get close to your inner child. This will allow you to get in touch with many of your likes and dislikes. As a Sagittarius, you are not always sure of what you want, so this is a good start. What did you enjoy as a child? What did you hate? This will bring you closer to your inner self. To get to know your inner child, ask yourself the questions you would likely ask someone on a first date. Answer them, as your seven-year-old self. I know it may be difficult to remember how you thought and felt as a child, but try your hardest!

Step 2: Pay attention to the lessons in every situation

Life as a Sagittarius can be quite dramatic. Don't worry; it's not always your fault. You probably find yourself in problematic situations quite often. Many people are very used to viewing these situations from a "why me?" perspective. When you do this, you are victimizing yourself. Re-wire your brain into recognizing that every downfall is a lesson. Once you pay attention to the lessons in each situation, you will be able to see the root of them. The root of these problems could be you. If it is, it's important that you figure that out.

Step 3: Ask loved ones to call you out on your behavior

Ask a friend or family member to call you out when you are behaving in a negative way. If you have recognized that you are quick-tempered, let a friend know to put you in your place when you are getting too angry, too quickly. Do not do this if you are not ready. If you can't handle being called out, wait until you are before you ask a friend to check you. The last thing you want to do is get mad at a friend for doing exactly what you asked them to do. When you are ready, you will find this very helpful. It will help you keep track of your behavior and recognize what your triggers may be.

Step 4: Check in with yourself every now and then

Being a Sagittarius, you are likely very busy. This means that you can get quite sidetracked in whatever it is that you are doing. Set an alarm on your phone for a daily mental check in. Check in with yourself, and see if you are actively working on being a better you throughout the day, whatever that means to you. It could be as simple as being kinder, practicing patience, or getting off social media. Whatever it is, remind yourself to check in so that you can hold yourself accountable. Eventually, you won't need this reminder, as this will become easier over time.

Zodiac Signs Unlocked: The Good

If there is one sign that gets along with everyone upon first impressions, it's the Sagittarius. Sagittarius is just one of those signs that everyone loves. They are kind and humble, yet extremely confident. People enjoy their presence, and they don't even know why. The interesting things about the Sagittarius is that they usually have a whole other side of them that many people don't know about.

I am extremely compatible with Sagittarius, so I usually get them to open up to me. This gives me access to a whole different side of the Sagittarius—the side that not many people see. One of my old coworkers opened up to me, and I found him to be the most interesting person. At work, he was known as the quiet, innocent, kind, and loving Paul. But the Paul that I knew was manipulative, secretive, angry, and malicious. It was very shocking to see how well he played both versions of himself. When dealing with a Sagittarius like this, usually this does not come out until they are extremely close to someone. We will dig deeper into that side later in this chapter. What you should know about the Sagittarius though, is that if you are looking for a loyal friend who will have your back through thick and thin, look no further! A Sagittarius friendship is like no other.

Sun: Wise, joyful, unapologetic, caring, fair, spiritual, honest, fun-loving

Moon: Sensitive, emotional, selfless, considerate, mature, positive, inspiring

Rising: Funny, relatable, understanding, open, freethinking, easygoing, fun

The Evolved Sagittarius

As an evolved Sagittarius, you are much more mature than average. If you are not yet at this stage, don't worry; you will be. You can expect to become one of the most considerate and selfless people to those around you. However, because of your no-nonsense attitude, people know better than to take advantage of you. The evolved Sagittarius knows boundaries. They are wise enough to know when something (or someone) is no longer serving them. Once they reach this point of self-awareness, it's almost like nothing gets past them. People learn not to take them for granted, which allows the Sagittarius to continue giving their love wholeheartedly.

Sagittarius is one of the most loyal signs. They will kill for you (I'm not kidding). If you are doing the inner work right now to become an evolved Sagittarius, you will blossom into a loving, caring, compassionate individual. You will also be very easy to be around. Sagittarius are so much fun! They are the life of the party, just like the Leo. As a Sagittarius, you will find many people drawn to your joyous energy. Trust your judgment and only let certain people in. Know when you are being paranoid vs. protective over your well-being. Once you learn the difference, your relationships will soar.

Zodiac Signs Unlocked: The Bad

The perfect way to describe a Sagittarius is "the sweetest bitch you will ever meet." Seriously. That's exactly what they are. They are loving, open, and kind, but in an instant they can turn into

Satan. Strong word choice? I'm sorry. It's the truth. When they tap into the negative side of their personality, it can get very ugly. If you are an unevolved Sagittarius, I suggest you make the effort be more mindful of some of your less favorable traits. I have provided you with some traits that shouldn't be considered a big deal, however, these traits can affect your relationships with others without you even realizing it.

Forgetful: If you are not someone they care deeply about, the Sagittarius is likely to be very forgetful with you. They will not pay attention to details, and will have a hard time keeping track of what is going on in your life. If you are a Sagittarius, it is very likely that you have a few people in your life that think you couldn't care less about them. This may be the furthest thing from the truth, but if you are constantly forgetting significant details or events, can you blame them for feeling this way?

Impatient: As a Sagittarius, you are probably extremely impatient. Because of this, you end up rushing into things, and getting bored quickly. For example, your impatience can cause you to settle on a job you may not like, simply because the hiring process was quick and easy. You jump in and out of relationships quickly, and you expect others to move at the same pace as you. Life can't always be on fast forward, Sagittarius. Take a moment to live in the present and you will find that you will experience much more enjoyment in life.

Sensitive: The Sagittarius can be overly sensitive at times. This mostly occurs in their romantic partnerships. They tend to get sensitive over minor things, and feel as if they have no control over it. The problem is, they don't always communicate this. They hold onto the emotions, thinking they will get over it, but instead, they just bottle it up. The truth usually comes out eventually, but it gets very ugly. If you are a Sagittarius, work through your emotions and communicate them to your partner. If you are sensitive, sometimes all you need is a little reassurance, and that's OK!

Zodiac Signs Unlocked: The Ugly

The toxic trait you need to be aware of: Possessiveness

How this affects my...

Relationships: Once people realize that you are controlling and possessive, they will distance themselves. You are pushing away the people you love because you try too hard to keep them close.

Productivity: You are so worried about the people you love, that you neglect other important areas in your life.

Mental state: Your inability to control others will affect your inner peace if you do not get it under control.

Digging Deeper...

Toxic trait: Possessiveness

The Sagittarius is a sign that is very loving. This is a great quality for the most part, however, at times it can be overbearing. They show affection in their own ways, and usually this includes being overly protective, possessive, and even obsessive at times. This side of the Sagittarius usually comes out with very close loved ones. They are overly protective, and will stop at nothing to make sure their loved ones are OK. Many times, they will be overbearing, and their loved ones get overwhelmed, which can eventually cause them to distance themselves.

If you are an unevolved Sagittarius, try your best to be self-aware enough so you will be able to recognize when you are behaving this way. Once you can recognize it, you can control it. Focus on controlling this toxic trait, rather than controlling those around you. It is not your job to protect those around you every second. Your loved ones will make mistakes, be mistreated, and interact with people that you may not think have the best intentions for them. Sometimes, you just have to let life happen to them, and be there for them when they need you.

Where Do I Begin?

I will tell you the same thing that I have told every single zodiac sign. Begin with the end in mind. Where do you see yourself at end of this mindfulness journey? Don't take the word "end" too seriously; this is a lifelong journey. It is important to understand where you see yourself after you have done all the crucial healing and inner work. That will keep you in alignment with your purpose. To understand your purpose, ask yourself the following three questions. These have all been customized to your moon sign. You can apply it to your sun sign as well.

1. Do I act out of emotion or logic? How can I find a balance?

2. Why do I allow others to dictate my happiness?

3. Am I too controlling over my loved ones? Does this push them away?

CHAPTER 10

The Capricorn

December 22-January 19

Ruling planet: Saturn   **Element:** Earth   **Symbol:** The Goat
Quality: Cardinal **Opposite sign:** Cancer

Self-Awareness

The good thing about being a Capricorn is that you probably already have the discipline it takes to commit to this journey to self-awareness and mindfulness. The first step is making the decision to make a change, and if you are reading this, you have already done that. Now it is time for execution. I'm guessing it probably took something bad in your life for this to happen.

Probably some sort of serious turn of event that forced you to wake up and realize that it is time to make major change in your life. It's OK; you'll get through it. It's time to put a plan into action. As a Capricorn, I know that is like music to your ears. You probably love a good plan.

Step 1: Come up with a plan

As mentioned, your zodiac sign loves to plan. It keeps you on track with whatever it is you are trying to achieve. In this case, it is self-awareness. Don't get me wrong though; in no way whatsoever do you need to feel obligated to stick to this plan. Think of it more as a guideline. This will keep you motivated to continue with this process. An example of a plan could be choosing certain days of the week to dedicate to self-care:

"I will journal every Monday, Wednesday, and Friday for half an hour. After this, I will meditate for twenty minutes, and read a few chapters of my favorite self-help book."

Whatever works for you! Don't be too hard on yourself if you can't commit. Do the best you can! This guideline will make it a little easier for you to stay on track!

Step 2: Experiment with different methods of self-discovery to see what works best for you

As a Capricorn, you have a particular way of doing things. In order to learn what type of self-reflection is best for you, I suggest you keep trying different methods to see what you enjoy the most. You can try recording yourself, journaling, writing letters to yourself, mediating, going for walks, bubble baths, painting, writing poetry—the possibilities are endless. Keep experimenting until you find one that feels right. One that doesn't feel like a chore. Once you find the method that is best for you, implement it into your daily routine.

Step 3: Don't be afraid to ask for help

Your loved ones are there to support you, whether you like it or not. I need you to realize that becoming self-aware is not easy. It is painful. You will uncover parts of yourself that you never knew existed, and not always good. In times like these, you will need support. Don't be afraid to reach out to people. I know you think you can handle everything on your own, and that you don't ever need help. The truth is, you do. Everyone does. So reach out to your friends, mom, dad, aunt, sibling, and ask for help. You'll feel better. Once you do, you can pick yourself back up, and continue to grow!

Step 4: Recognize that there is no right or wrong way to do this.

Everyone's experience is unique. Do not put pressure on yourself. If you told yourself that you will journal ten pages a day, but you can only write two today, don't force yourself to push out eight more pages just to meet your goal. If you do this, you are turning it into a chore. Mindfulness is not a chore. It is a choice. You are choosing to do this inner work, and that is a beautiful thing, so enjoy it! Yes, it might hurt like hell at times, and you may find yourself crying more often, but you will come out on top. There is light at the end of the tunnel, and you are evolving into the person you're meant to be, so keep going!

Zodiac Signs Unlocked: The Good

As a Capricorn, you are known to be one of the most reliable signs of the zodiac. If you say you will be there, you mean it. You don't go back on your word. You come off as reserved, and even boring at times, but anyone that gets to know you on a deeper level will say that you are one of the most entertaining people they know. Not everyone gets to see this side of you, but the people that do are bound to stick around. There is never a dull moment with you.

Sun: Charming, entertaining, loyal, patient, attractive, conventional, respectful

Moon: Generous, helpful, kind, empathetic, calculated, fearless, concerned

Rising: Reserved, profound, responsible, adaptable, dependable, organized, well-mannered

The Evolved Capricorn

A Capricorn that is evolved is one of those signs that surprises many people. Many have the assumption that you are boring and reserved. I'll be honest; I was one of those people. Capricorns are more than meets the eye. Behind the responsible, practical, conventional Capricorn is a fun, loving, and carefree Capricorn. Your sign is actually one of the most entertaining of them all. There is never a dull moment with a witty Capricorn. They are so charming.

I remember I fell for this guy in college that I wasn't physically attracted to AT ALL, simply because of his Capricorn charm. He was goofy and witty, and I was all over it! Don't get me wrong; the practical and responsible Capricorn is not a façade. You really are that diverse. You know the difference between work and play, and do a great job at maintaining a balance. Well, most of you do.

There are, of course, the unevolved Capricorns whose personalities would contradict many of these traits, but it's OK, we are all there once. The evolved Capricorn is someone that is very easy to be around. Contrary to popular belief, Capricorns have a very sensitive and loving side to them. In fact, they can get quite mushy sometimes in romantic relationships (I know, very hard to imagine). You guys do such a great job at keeping up this tough persona, but I know what lies beneath the surface, and it's great!

Zodiac Signs Unlocked: The Bad

Selfish: If you are not close to a Capricorn, they can be some of the most selfish people you will ever meet. They are very prideful, and do not like to ask for any type of help, so they expect the same from others. If you do not have a close relationship with a Capricorn, you will find that they are very greedy and selfish with you. They're the type of people that refuse to catch you up on what you missed in class while you were sick, just because. In their mind, if they can make something possible, so can everyone else. They have the "every man for himself" mentality. If you are an unevolved Capricorn, I suggest you make the effort be more mindful of some of your less favorable traits. I have provided you with some traits that shouldn't be considered a big deal, however, these traits can affect your relationships with others without you even realizing it.

Pessimistic: The Capricorn is known to be a realist. They look at things from a very logical perspective and they can detach their emotions from most situations. Because of this, they can be quite pessimistic. In their mind, they believe that by viewing life this way, they can avoid disappointment. However, what they fail to realize is that when they are pessimistic they are emitting negative energy, therefore attracting more negativity. Lighten up Capricorn. Expect the best.

Judgmental: Because the Capricorn is such a grounded and practical sign, they can be very judgmental of others who choose not to live their life this way. They can be very expressive and they do not hold back when giving their opinions. Their opinions are usually biased, because they believe that others should live by their own personal beliefs. This causes them to appear extremely judgmental, even if that is not their intent.

Zodiac Signs Unlocked: The Ugly

The toxic trait you need to be aware of: Close-mindedness

How this affects my...

Relationships: You have a hard time seeing your loved-ones' perspectives when you are in a disagreement.

Productivity: You stick to what you know, even if there can be a faster, more efficient way of getting things done. You are not open to advice that may really help you.

Mental state: You may not see the brighter side of things because you are too focused on what you know and believe.

Digging Deeper...

Toxic trait: Closed-mindedness

The Capricorn likes to live their life in a very particular way. They usually have habits and routines that they have kept up with for years. They do not have a strong desire to change, as they are pretty content staying in their comfort zone. I have an old friend that has the same routine every day. This includes eating the same breakfast, walking her dog at a scheduled time, and sticking to a strict bedtime—even on weekends. They like to keep things in their life very predictable. If you consider yourself to be an unevolved Capricorn, it is likely that you struggle with being quite closed-minded. Life is very black and white for you, so you have a hard time understanding the ways in which other people choose to live their lives. You can be very judgmental of other people, and you don't see any problem with this.

As a Capricorn, it is important that you become more open-minded. You are missing out on a lot of great people and experiences due to your preconceived notions. Make an effort to try new things. For example, trying new foods, traveling to destinations you've never considered, or even dating someone who is not your usual type! Stepping out of your comfort zone is important for your growth. You will learn that you find a lot more enjoyment out of life.

Where Do I Begin?

I will tell you the same thing that I have told every single zodiac sign. Begin with the end in mind. Where do you see yourself at end of this mindfulness journey? Don't take the word "end" too seriously; this is a lifelong journey. It is important to understand where you see yourself after you have done all the crucial healing and inner work. That will keep you in alignment with your purpose. To understand your purpose, ask yourself the following three questions. These have all been customized to your moon sign. You can apply it to your sun sign as well.

1. Why do I find a problem in every solution?

2. Do I need to spend more time listening to others?

3. How can I learn to be more open-minded?

CHAPTER 11

The Aquarius

January 20-February 18

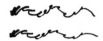

Ruling planet: Uranus/Saturn ♅ / ♄ **Element:** Air △
Symbol: The Water Bearer ≈≈ **Quality:** Fixed **Opposite sign:** Leo

Self-Awareness

Ahh, Aquarius, one of the most misunderstood signs. Also, one of the most difficult zodiac signs. (I'm allowed to say that, I'm an Aquarius.) You probably thought you were self-aware, until life hit you in the face and forced you to realize that you aren't. For some reason, extreme events need to occur for you to decide to make a change in your life. You are probably going through something right now, and ended up getting this book because you finally came to terms with certain aspects of yourself that you are not proud of. I'm sorry you had to learn the hard way, but you are here now. If you've hit rock bottom, just know there is literally nowhere to go but up. Good things are coming.

Step 1: Get in tune with your spirituality

Aquarius are kind of known as the hippies of the zodiac. Usually, Aquarius are the ones who are spiritually in tune. Create a spiritual self-care routine. Since I am an Aquarius, I will share mine. Hopefully, it will inspire you.

Every day, I set aside an hour each night to dedicate to my self-care routine. I immerse myself in a crystal sound bath (thanks YouTube), light a green candle (green is associated with your heart chakra), journal, say my affirmations, pray, meditate, talk to my archangels, put lavender oil on my pulse points to relax, drink a large glass of water, and dance to one song. I do this every night before bed.

The reason why I am telling you this, is because the more I practice this, the more sacred it becomes to me. I am able to give myself the love and affection I need. The more I love myself, the more I want to improve myself. Once you establish self-love, you will want to get to know yourself better so that you can improve!

Step 2: Ask yourself thought-provoking questions

If the questions make you nervous, even better! Find some thought-provoking questions (there are some at the beginning of this book), and answer them. If the questions don't make you uncomfortable, find better ones. These questions should make you second guess who you are. As an Aquarius, you like to be challenged. A good exercise is to answer the questions at the beginning of the month, then again at the end of the month. Compare the two, and see the growth. Continue to follow up with yourself so that you can keep track of your progress, not matter how painful it may be!

Step 3: Record yourself talking though your problems

This one sounds a little strange, I know. As an Aquarius, you often feel misunderstood. There are many times that you want to vent to your friend, but don't, because you know that requires explaining your entire thought process which is virtually impossible. Recording yourself talking through your problems is oddly therapeutic. I know it sounds crazy, but TRY IT. When you record yourself, you will feel as though what you say has been given purpose. Your words will flow freely. You know that this video has intent behind it so your thoughts will come out very naturally. It will feel as though you are venting to a friend on FaceTime, except they're super quiet. This video will feel like an emotional release, and you will feel better after recording it. Whether you watch it or not won't make much of a difference.

Step 4: Write down every time you go back to old habits

I'll give you an example. Let's say you are trying to stop being so damn hypocritical, every time you catch yourself being a hypocrite, write it down in your notes app. Write down the whole situation.

Example: Today I was a hypocrite when I got upset with my brother for not driving me to work, when I refused him a ride last week.

Once you've compiled a list, read it back and analyze it to find common themes. Is there a repeated pattern in each situation? This will make it easier for you to narrow down the root cause of your behaviors, and why you act a certain way in given situations. You will find this to be extremely helpful in your self-awareness journey, trust me! Whatever you do, don't give up. Even when you feel as though you have done enough inner work. There is no such thing as "enough." We are constantly growing and evolving and need to maintain healthy relationships with ourselves to excel in life. This is a lifelong journey. Enjoy it!

Zodiac Signs Unlocked: The Good

Oh, Aquarius...I have a special place in my heart for you. Mostly, because I am an Aquarius, (and proud of it). We are one of the most complicated signs of the zodiac, mostly because we are always on both extreme ends of one spectrum. For example, we can be extremely open-minded, but also the most stubborn people on the planet. How does this work? Aquarius is a very interesting sign. I say this because you never know what to expect when you are dealing with an Aquarius. They are full of surprises, and it's always a crazy ride.

Sun: Logical, caring, understanding, open-minded, carefree, weird, eccentric, sarcastic, hilarious, refreshing

Moon: Sensitive, practical, fair, great communication, loving, affectionate, expressive, creative, spiritual

Rising: Introverted, happy, positive, free, inventive, carefree, unbothered, self-aware, unapologetic, smart

The Evolved Aquarius

The evolved Aquarius is an unstoppable force. Remember when I said an Aquarius is on the extreme end of either side of a spectrum? Well, here's the thing. When an Aquarius is unevolved, they can be extremely toxic, but once they are evolved, they blossom into an amazing person. They are practical and loving. The "cold-hearted Aquarius" stereotype does not exist in this Aquarius. They love deeply and will do a lot for the people they care about. They are extremely loyal and giving in relationships. They are constantly working on themselves to become their best self. They are hard workers, and will do anything to achieve their wildest dreams.

An evolved Aquarius is likely to be living their purpose, and chasing their dreams at all times. They will stop at nothing to get what they want. They are out of the ordinary, and usually their dreams are unconventional. They have high standards for themselves and others, but are also realistic in the goals they set. The evolved Aquarius is one of the most carefree and liberated signs. They march to the beat of their own drum, and they don't care who is watching. If you need a friend to get you out of your comfort zone, stick to an Aquarius. They make it seem so easy; you won't even realize you're doing it. Expect the unexpected with them.

Zodiac Signs Unlocked: The Bad

The Aquarius marches to the beat of their own drum. They don't spend much time concerned with the opinions of others. This sounds like a good thing, but it can get a little toxic. The unevolved Aquarius can be quite inconsiderate and self-involved. If you are an unevolved Aquarius, I suggest you make the effort be more mindful of some of your less favorable traits. I have provided you with some traits that shouldn't be considered a big deal, however, these traits can affect your relationships with others without you even realizing it.

Bossy: The Aquarius likes things done a certain way. "My way or the highway" is a mentality that many of them have. If you are close to an Aquarius, you've probably experienced their bossy side. They tend to order others around, and expect people to stop what they are doing to tend to their needs. They can be very entitled. If you work with an Aquarius, you are likely to experience this side of them. It can be very nasty. If you are an Aquarius, I can guess that you are already aware of this trait. Just because people don't speak up, doesn't mean it does not bother them. Be mindful of this trait. Don't be that person.

Absentminded: The unevolved Aquarius is very unorganized. Their mind is a chaotic mess, and it runs a mile a minute. They have a hard time keeping track of what is going on in their life, and this can get very frustrating. The absentminded Aquarius is very forgetful, and can barely hold a conversation. You will notice that they often zone out of interactions, and it often seems like their mind is somewhere else. If you are an Aquarius, this isn't cute or quirky. TRUST me. Learn how to be fully present in the moment.

Sensitive: The Aquarius likes to pretend that they are a cold-hearted robot, but they are actually extremely sensitive. They take things very personally, and sometimes they feel like they have no control over this. As an Aquarius, you may find that you are easily affected by the words of others. A lot of times, this has to do with a lack of confidence. A confident Aquarius is very secure, and is not as sensitive as the unevolved Aquarius. Your sensitivity will decrease once you work on practicing self-love. You will become unfazed by the words and actions of others. If you have a hard time working on your confidence, pay attention to your thoughts. You tend to overthink much more than you should. You have a habit of twisting people's words, without asking them what they really meant.

Zodiac Signs Unlocked: The Ugly

The toxic trait you need to be aware of: Self-interestedness

How this affects my...

Relationships: Many people get tired of catering to your needs when it is not reciprocated.

Productivity: You are so set in your ways that you have a hard time viewing the bigger picture. This could cause you to go down the wrong path in life.

Mental state: You are too critical of yourself even if you are doing well.

Digging Deeper...

Toxic Trait: Self-interestedness

The unevolved Aquarius can be a very difficult sign to know and love. They can be very self-interested, and have a hard time reciprocating the love and kindness shown to them. They have high expectations of others, but can't meet these expectations themselves. The problem with the unevolved Aquarius is that they are not self-aware enough to know that they are doing this. In their mind, they're making an effort. However, what they fail to realize is that they usually make the most effort when it is somehow beneficial for them.

If you are an unevolved Aquarius, take a second to consider what you put into your relationships (whether platonic or romantic), and what you get in return. Do you find that you are constantly asking your loved ones to be better in your relationships, but fail to work on yourself and recognize your own flaws? The Aquarius can be so focused on themselves that they often don't realize that they are mistreating loved ones. Be very aware of this, Aquarius! You will see how much your relationships improve. Trust me.

Where Do I Begin?

I will tell you the same thing that I have told every single zodiac sign. Begin with the end in mind. Where do you see yourself at end of this mindfulness journey? Don't take the word 'end' too seriously; this is a lifelong journey. It is important to understand where you see yourself after you have done all the crucial healing and inner work. That will keep you in alignment with your purpose. To understand your purpose, ask yourself the following three questions. These have all been customized to your moon sign. You can apply it to your sun sign as well.

1.   Why do I feel the need to make everything about myself? How can I change this?

2.   Why do I have the tendency to be so hypocritical? What causes this?

3.   Am I defensive, and why?

CHAPTER 12

The Pisces

February 19-March 20

Ruling planet: Neptune/Jupiter ♆ /♃ **Element:** Water ▽
Symbol: The Fish ♓ **Quality:** Mutable **Opposite sign:** Virgo

Self-Awareness

I am so proud of you Pisces. I know it wasn't easy for you to make the decision to change your life. Many of you live in your own little bubble. I call it "Pisces dreamland." This is where you reside. In Pisces dreamland, everything is perfect. Everything is OK. All the issues you have are swept under a rug that is to never be lifted. If you picked up this book, that means you have lifted the rug, and you are ready to sweep all the shit out from under it. You have finally decided to leave your dreamland, and come face to face with reality.

Step 1: Find a creative outlet

As a Pisces, I know there is something you are quite skilled in. If you haven't yet discovered it, then try new things until you find something you are passionate about. Most of you are creative in some way, whether you sing, write, take photographs, play an instrument, or dance. Find what you are passionate about, and use it as an emotional release. You are an extremely sensitive and emotional water sign, and if you don't have an emotional release, you will probably end up hurting a loved one because you are keeping so much bottled up.

Step 2: Allow the people close to you to get to know your inner self

Pisces often keep a major part of their personality to themselves. This is the darker, mysterious side of the Pisces. The side that no one knows exists until things get bad. Usually, the Pisces seems to be the most innocent, carefree, easygoing sign of the zodiac. Deep down, there is a dark side. I know you know what I'm talking about. The one that stays locked alone in your room overthinking things you wouldn't say out loud. Usually, when you upset a Pisces, this side is slightly revealed, which is why an angry Pisces is so toxic. My advice to you: show your loved ones the good and the bad. This way, when shit hits the fan, your words aren't as hurtful, and your emotions aren't as intense. This will go a long way.

Step 3: Stop feeling sorry for yourself

One of the main reasons that you, Pisces, may not begin
your journey to mindfulness is because you have a hard
time acknowledging that you have the ability to change your
situation. You can choose to be happy. You can choose to raise
your vibrations; you just have to *make* this choice. Get out of
dreamland and recognize that life is happening around you
whether you like it or not! (I'm sorry if I sound harsh, but if anyone
needs this bluntness, it's you!) When you make the choice to stop
feeling sorry for yourself, you will see things clearer.

I remember an old friend of mine spent five years working on
getting her degree. Every year she would change her major, and
take fewer and fewer classes so that she had an easier workload.
No matter what she did, she couldn't seem to figure out why she
had such a hard time in school. What should've taken three years
had taken her almost six. This is because she refused to wake up
and face the reality that maybe school just wasn't for her! Maybe
she wanted a job that doesn't require an education and that's OK!
What's not OK is spending $40,000 of the government's money
to come to a decision you could've made if you stepped into
reality. You will learn how to accept your situation, adapt to it, and
change it. Get out of your comfort zone.

Step 4: Express gratitude

I mentioned raising your vibrations in step 3. To raise your
vibrations means to shift your energy into a more positive state,
for your benefit. One way of doing this is to express gratitude

as often as you can. I suggest practicing this daily. At the end of every day, write three things you are grateful for. It can be as simple as "I woke up today." Seriously. That's a huge deal. The more you express gratitude, the more appreciation you will have for life. Once you have this appreciation, it will spark into the desire for change, and happiness. This will go a long way for you as a Pisces. As someone who is constantly in tune with your emotions, don't you want to feel good more often? You deserve it Pisces! Make it happen.

Zodiac Signs Unlocked: The Good

Last, but certainly not least, Pisces! You are a special zodiac sign. The Pisces is one of the most emotional and expressive signs. You are usually quite creative, and extremely intuitive. I like to think that every Pisces is a little psychic, and many even choose to be spiritually in tune. Pisces gravitate toward anything taboo. Their curious nature draws them toward the unknown, and this is one thing that makes this sign so fascinating. Pisces are lovable, kind, and always have an open heart. Being around a Pisces is like being around a childhood friend, even if you just met them. They are one of the friendliest signs of the zodiac.

Sun: Talkative, imaginative, loving, generous, friendly, charming, romantic

Moon: Emotional, sensitive, loveable, caring, considerate, spiritual, comforting, creative

↑ **Rising:** Helpful, compassionate, understanding, talkative, wise, open-minded, calm

The Evolved Pisces

The evolved Pisces is usually very in tune with their emotions and state of awareness. Self-awareness is quite difficult to master as a Pisces, so when they do, it can be magical. Once the Pisces is able to understand their flaws, strengths, weaknesses, etc., they are able to transform into the beautiful beings that they are.

My favorite singer and poet, Jhené Aiko (a Pisces), once said, "I love all the layers that a Pisces has. I can adapt to any situation, to any part of the world, anything. I feel like there's nothing that I'm afraid of. I don't know if it's because I'm a Pisces, or if it's the way I grew up, but I feel like Pisces are very well-rounded. But you know, every sign has its good and its bad." I've always found this to be true. They can be extremely caring and considerate. They are loving and nurturing. You will never question if a Pisces loves you. Their love is as deep as the ocean (haha, get the water sign and fish reference there?). Seriously though, I don't know if there is a love like the love of the evolved Pisces.

The evolved Pisces is patient, and understanding. They are able to recognize a problem before it gets out of hand. They are not afraid of confrontation, and are able to be open and honest with their loved ones, and their selves. The Pisces is always said to be a dreamer. Their imagination is admirable, and this is one of the reasons why many of them are so creative. An evolved Pisces is able to turn their pain into something beautiful. You, or a Pisces you know, are likely to be involved with some sort of art. Whether it is painting, singling, dancing, drawing, or playing an instrument, the Pisces is always creating something beautiful. As you evolve and grow, you will likely find a way to turn your pain into something beautiful as well. If you're a Pisces, you're probably in your feelings 90 percent of the time, so you may as well find an emotional outlet.

Zodiac Signs Unlocked: The Bad

The Pisces is one of those signs that you can't help but love. However, once you get close to them, you experience a whole new side of them. Beneath their loving and innocent exterior, there is a darker, less pleasant person. The unevolved Pisces can be quite critical, manipulative, and depressive. If you are an unevolved Pisces, I suggest you make the effort be more mindful of some of your less favorable traits. I have provided you with some traits that shouldn't be considered a big deal, however, these traits can affect your relationships with others without you even realizing it.

Overly emotional: It is no secret that the Pisces is emotional. They are a water sign, and they take things to heart. Usually, a situation will be over dramatized in their mind. They are heavily affected by anything and everything. They feel empathy for others very deeply, and this can cause them to spiral into a whirlwind of thoughts that brings them back to their own personal issues. It is important for a Pisces to surround themselves with positive and happy people, due to the fact that they take on other people's emotions as their own. If you are a Pisces, be careful about who you have around you.

Self-pitying: The unevolved Pisces can be extremely self-pitying. I like to think it's because it helps them cope with life better. They have this victim mentality in which life is always happening to them, not for them. They have a hard time seeing the bigger picture and often get themselves stuck in a depressive "woe is me" state. They don't make much effort to change their situations; instead, they have a pity party all alone and hope that things will magically get better. As a Pisces, make an effort to get out of this victim mentality. You will be much happier.

Insecure: Due to the fact that the Pisces is constantly stuck in their own thoughts, they can become quite insecure. They overthink simple things that don't hold much value. They spend a lot of time over-analyzing their interactions with others, right down to their tone of voice and their facial expressions. Because of the fact that they can be so critical of themselves, they believe that people around them think the same way, when in reality, no one cares about what they said or didn't say. The only one who cares is you, Pisces. So try to get out of your own head, and be nicer to yourself.

Zodiac Signs Unlocked: The Ugly

The toxic trait you need to be aware of: Putting others before yourself

How this affects my...

Relationships: People will take advantage of you and you might not even realize it.

Productivity: When you love someone, they become your world. You will find that you neglect the things that are important to you.

Mental state: You are too focused on making sure others are happy, so you do not prioritize your own needs.

Digging Deeper...

Toxic Trait: Putting others before yourself

As a Pisces, you are such a loving and caring individual, that you have a habit of putting others' needs before your own. You are so focused on making sure that the people you love are happy, that you neglect your own happiness. As an unevolved Pisces, it is important to realize that your own glass has to be full before you can start pouring it out into others. Taking care of yourself needs to become your priority, otherwise you will get into the Pisces depressive state, which isn't pretty. You can't help everyone, Pisces. It is important that you recognize when you are prioritizing others. If you are not emotionally available to others because you have your own emotions to deal with, that is OK. Disappointing others is OK if it means putting yourself first. Once you are full of self-love, you will be able to love others in a healthy way. Once you do this, you will find your relationships much more fulfilling, rather than draining. Trust me!

Where Do I Begin?

I will tell you the same thing that I have told every single zodiac sign. Begin with the end in mind. Where do you see yourself at end of this mindfulness journey? Don't take the word "end" too seriously; this is a lifelong journey. It is important to understand where you see yourself after you have done all the crucial healing and inner work. That will keep you in alignment with your purpose. To understand your purpose, ask yourself the following three questions. These have all been customized to your moon sign. You can apply it to your sun sign as well.

1. Why is it that I am so willing to put others before myself?

2. Do I take things too personally, and why?

3. Am I the cause of my unhappiness?

CHAPTER 13
Zodiac Mindfulness

Imagine that you are already living as the best version of yourself. How does it feel? What does this dream life look like?

These are important things to visualize as you navigate through this journey to mindfulness. Not only is visualization important, but claiming this dream life as if it is already yours will go a long way as well. I practice doing this by reciting affirmations daily. Affirmations are an important part of my morning and nightly routine. The more you say something, the more you believe it. The more you feel it. The more you become it. Trust me. Affirmations will go a long way. You will be emitting that positive energy of what you desire out into the universe, and the universe is bound to give it back to you! In case you're confused, an affirmation is pretty much just a positive statement to help you overcome any negative thoughts. Some of my affirmations include:

> I am the woman of my dreams.
> I love myself inside and out.
> I am living the life of my dreams.
> I make amazing money doing what I love.

I am living my purpose.
Everything that I desire is currently manifesting.

These affirmations help me in many ways. They are a positive reinforcement that motivates and inspires me to become the best version of myself. I know it might sound like a whole lot of bullshit. I also know that doing this for the first time can be quite awkward. The first time I did it, I felt ridiculous! I remember sitting in my room at 2 a.m., saying my affirmations out loud to myself in the mirror. I felt like I was taking to myself, and if I'm being honest, it felt pointless. The thing is, I had promised myself I would try it out for seven days, no matter how ridiculous it felt. I'd try it for a week, and if I felt a difference, I would keep going.

Two years later, I'm still saying them every day (twice a day) and preaching about it in this book. Saying affirmations changed my life. Not only were they reminders of all the things I wanted to accomplish and become, but the more I said them, the more they became my reality! Seriously. Every few months, I have to add new affirmations because the old ones have been accomplished. I no longer have to tell myself I am self-aware, or that I am independent! Affirmations work like a charm. Try it for seven days and see the difference it will make in your life. You will feel more positive, and you'll be less likely to take part in negative self-talk.

In this chapter, I have created a short list of affirmations, based on what areas I think your zodiac sign needs improvement in. I suggest you use you look at your sun, moon, and rising sign's affirmations. That means fifteen affirmations for seven days. I believe in you! Say these out loud in the mirror before you start your day. Make eye contact with yourself, say them with force, and try your hardest to believe them as you say them! The more emotion you put behind them, the more effective they will be. I understand it can be awkward at first, so don't be too hard on yourself if you find it uncomfortable. If you have roommates or family members you don't want to hear, you can say it in your mind's eye, but if you have the opportunity to say them out loud, it will make a huge difference!

Once you get into the habit of declaring these affirmations, find ways to incorporate this practice into your daily routine. For example, whenever I warm up my car in the winter, I take that time to say my affirmations in my tiny little car mirror. There's no such thing as having no time. This is your mental health. Prioritize it!

Affirmations

Aries

I am selfless.
I think before I react.
I am in control of my emotions.
I am considerate.
I am self-aware.

Taurus

The only person's opinion that holds value to me is my own.
I am open-minded.
I am productive.
I do things wholeheartedly, and have no expectations from others.
I am fair.

Gemini

I am 100 percent myself around others.
I am rational.
I am kind.
I am present.
I treat others the way I want to be treated.

Cancer

I put myself first.
I love myself inside and out.
I am secure.
I am enough. My effort is enough. My love is enough.
I am confident.

Leo

I am not concerned with the opinions of others.
I know my worth.
I am kind.
The only validation I need is my own.
I only attract good things.

Virgo

I am perfect the way that I am.
I am impeccable with my word.
I am honest.
I am whole.
I love myself.

Libra

I am all that I need.
I am fearless.
I am independent.
I am self-reliant.
I love myself inside and out.

Scorpio

I allow good things to happen to me.
My heart is open to love.
I am enough.
I am confident and secure.
I put myself first.

Sagittarius

I am secure.
I am patient.
I prioritize myself.
I know my worth.
I am in control of my emotions.

Capricorn

I am open to love.
I am open-minded.
I am optimistic.
Good things happen to me.
I am selfless.

Aquarius

I am living the life of my dreams.
I am selfless.
I am the best version of myself.
I am fair.
I love myself.

Pisces

I put myself first.
I love myself more than I love anyone else.
I am in tune with reality.
I am secure.
I am amazing and irreplaceable.

Journal Challenge

Find the affirmations according to your sun, moon, and rising signs, and recite fifteen affirmations daily for seven days! Write about your experience daily (it can be two to three sentences). See how your life changes!

Day 1

Day 2

Day 3

Day 4

Day 5

Day 6

Day 7

CHAPTER 14

Self-Care Practices

As this book comes to an end, I really want to make sure you get the most out of reading it. I understand it can be difficult to do inner work. We always feel like we don't have time, and living as we do feels comfortable, so why disrupt that? I want you to understand that when you prioritize yourself, you *will* find the time. And because I want to make extra sure that you gain benefit out of this book, I'm going to leave you with a final summary of the techniques I mentioned (and some new ones) that helped me on this journey. You can choose to do all ten, or pick whichever resonate with you. You do not need to have your zodiac sign in mind when picking a technique. These will benefit anyone! I understand we all have busy lives, so try to find the ones that work best for you and your lifestyle.

1. Decide to work on yourself

I know this sounds simple, but hear me out. We can literally do anything we set our minds to. We are the only ones standing in the way of our own success. When beginning this journey, it's important that you make the decision to commit to it. If that means waking up twenty minutes earlier so that you can practice a self-care routine every morning, find a way to make it happen! The journey to mindfulness is not something that another person can do for you. You are in control of your own life. If you don't take action, no one will. Make the decision to do the inner work, and understand that making that decision means committing to it. If you are not ready to commit, do not expect results. There is no way to sugarcoat this. Either you want this for yourself, or you don't.

2. Learn how to raise your vibrations

This is not something that I mentioned too often in the book, but it is something that has helped me out a lot throughout my journey. There are days when I don't feel the greatest. I wake up in a bad mood, and nothing seems to excite me. In these times, I make the choice to raise my vibrations. If this is an unfamiliar concept to you, raising your vibrations means that you are raising your energetic frequency (or to put it simply, putting yourself in a better mood). I do this by taking five deep breaths, and making sure to smile as a I breathe out. On my last breath I say out loud "I am raising my vibrations." You can also do this silently in your mind if you are in public. Tell yourself that you are raising your vibrations, and allow your emotions to flow for a few moments. It works! Trust me.

3. Meditate

Meditation is super important to me. I do it every single day, sometimes even multiple times a day. Adding meditation into your daily routine can and will change your life. Even if you only have time for a ten-minute meditation, that is enough! Find a meditation routine that works for you. If you have trouble focusing, I suggest looking up guided meditations online, or even finding relaxation music on your favorite streaming app. My favorite way to meditate is by listening to someone playing singing bowls online, or by playing a guided meditation. Always make sure to find a comfortable position, and make sure you have no distractions. I suggest creating a peaceful environment. You can do this by dimming the lights, lighting a candle or incense, or putting your favorite scent in your diffuser. Do whatever you need to do to get the most out of your meditation experience.

4. Eliminate negative self-talk

As I mentioned, negative self-talk is one of the worst things you can do to yourself. If you don't have it in you to be positive all the time, I get it. I'm just telling you not to be negative. Remember that saying "If you don't have anything nice to say, don't say it at all"? Apply it to yourself! If you can't sit in the mirror and tell yourself you're beautiful, fine! Just don't tell yourself that you are ugly. Negative self-talk will attract more negative energy, and will totally lower your vibration. Avoid this at all costs! Once you've done the inner work, hopefully you will find it in yourself to tell yourself that you are beautiful every damn day!

5. Remove toxic people and environments from your life

In life, we have choices. No matter how many people try to make us feel like we don't, we absolutely do. In every situation. If you don't like your job, leave. If you have toxic friends, cut them off. I don't care if you've known them for ten years, or if you don't think you'll find a job anywhere else. Life will go on. You will adapt. Make the changes necessary in your life to ensure that you are only around positivity. If that means cutting off your best friend of ten years because your relationship with them no longer serves you, do what needs to be done! Once you remove all the toxic baggage, you will begin to attract greatness! These toxic people and environments are holding you back. This could be your job, friends, family, or even your living situation. We all have choices, so make the choice to do what is best for you.

6. Express gratitude

Expressing gratitude is one of the best ways to attract positivity into your life. It will remind you of all the good things that surround you. Have you ever taken a second to acknowledge that the lifestyle you currently live could be the one you were praying for just a few years ago? Take the time to be grateful for that. Every morning, before I even open my eyes, I tell myself three things that I am grateful for. Every single morning. If I can't think of any, I'll keep it as simple as "I'm grateful I woke up this morning" because that is a gift! Expressing gratitude is a way of raising your vibrations! Why wouldn't you want to start your day off like that? When you are feeling low, remind yourself of the things that you are grateful for. Keep lists in your phone, or say it out loud. Whatever works for you.

7. Practice affirmations

As I mentioned, affirmations are a great way to remind yourself of the amazing person that you are! Whether you believe the affirmations or not, every time you say them, they are planting a seed in your subconscious mind. I will say though, the more you say them, the more you will believe and become them. Take the time every day to recite your affirmations. Whether it be out loud, or in your mind, whatever works for you. I say mine every morning and night in the mirror, and this is what works best for me. You will find your own routine, and it will be perfect. If you don't know where to start, return to chapter 13 to find fifteen affirmations to recite daily.

8. Commit to a self-care routine

If you don't know where to begin your journey, start by showing yourself the love and affection you deserve. Put aside time for yourself, the same way you would for a romantic partner, or close friend. Dedicate at least thirty to forty minutes a day to a self-love routine. Whether this means reading your favorite book, journaling about your day, meditating, or some self-reflection while in the bath. Take the time to nourish yourself. Add on to your routine as often as you can, and prioritize your own well-being. If you are someone that finds yourself mindlessly scrolling though social media for hours at a time, replace your screen time with your self-care routine. We all think we don't have time, but we do. We just have to make ourselves a priority. Worry about yourself before you worry about strangers on social media. This will go a long way!

9. Journal

Journaling is one of the best ways to get to know yourself on a deeper level. When you journal, you are able to keep track of where your mind is at in that moment. Have you ever read your old high school journals and laughed at how immature you were? I know I have. Trust me when I tell you that if you are doing the inner work, the journal entries you write today will have you laughing in embarrassment next year. And that's a great thing! You will see the growth and you will feel so proud. You will also laugh at how ridiculous you were, but embrace it. Journaling is also a great way to release any pent-up emotions that you don't feel comfortable sharing with others. It's like an emotional cleanse. I suggest journaling a few thoughts every morning, and committing to a more intensive entry at nighttime.

10. Keep track of progress and help friends

As previously mentioned, take the time to ask your loved ones to give you updates on your journey. When you feel as though you have made progress, ask your friends if they've noticed. It is a great way to keep you motivated. Your loved ones can also be helpful by calling you out when you are mistreating them. If you tell them to let you know when you are behaving a certain way, you will be more likely to notice it yourself in the future. The more they call you out, the more self-aware you will become. Eventually, you won't need them to tell you anymore.

Now that I have given you ten different techniques to achieve mindfulness, you have no excuses! Begin your journey, and become the best version of yourself. We have been given a cheat code through the stars; it's time we use it! Your zodiac sign is not just here to tell you if you and your crush will work out; it's here to be a guide to achieve inner peace and mindfulness.

If you've made it this far, I am extremely proud of you. I know that getting to know yourself can be difficult. Beginning the journey to self-awareness is one of the most beautiful, yet painful experiences I've ever had. You learn all the shitty aspects of your personality, and that hurts. But once you realize you can correct your behavior, and even better, realize your progress, you begin to cherish yourself. You start to view life differently.

Picture it this way. You spend months discovering yourself. You're finally at a place in which you can say that you are self-aware, so now you have discovered all your dark sides. You spend months crying, healing, and overcoming childhood trauma. You are now working on correcting your behavior, and bettering yourself. You've finally reached a place of self-love, and it feels glorious. No one can knock you down; no one can tell you that you are not enough. You know what you're worth now, and that you are one of a kind. You're untouchable, and it feels great. You will get there, I promise you. You just have to do the work. No one is going to do this for you. It doesn't matter how many videos you watch, how many quotes you read, or how many appointments with your therapist you attend. If you do not do the work on yourself, these tools mean nothing. Even this book means nothing. Do the work. You'll love yourself for it, I promise.

FINAL THOUGHTS

Wow, you did it! You made it to the end. From the bottom of my heart, I truly do hope that this book helped you out. I hope that you use the tools and techniques provided to better yourself. I understand the journey can be difficult, but it is so worth it. I've had multiple breakdowns, depressive months, and buckets of tears, but here I am today, writing this book. I hope that by sharing my experiences, I can inspire someone to begin their journey to mindfulness.

I also want to point out that I began my journey without even considering my astrological placements. I didn't even think to use my sign as a cheat code, so consider yourself lucky! You really do have the entire universe to guide you through this process, so you better use it! Before I end this book, I want to leave you with a few thoughts that hold a lot of significance to me.

Sometimes, when we are not fully aligned with our higher self, it's hard to go after the things we love and are passionate about. It was only when I decided to better myself (spiritually, emotionally, physically) that my YouTube channel, *The Amateur Guru*, had really begun to take off! The channel led me to owning my own business at twenty-two years old and writing a book at twenty-four! If it weren't for all the internal work that I did, I probably wouldn't be here today. As an Aquarius, I have many thoughts, so I hope you don't mind that I go off on a little tangent right now.

Being a person of color, specifically a Black/Latina (my Aquarius father is Jamaican, and my Leo mother is Salvadoran), the odds are not always in my favor. Getting on such a large platform such as YouTube can be very intimidating. Especially when most of its viewership is, to put it simply, white. My thumbnails always had to be more interesting, my videos had to be longer, and I always had to think outside the box to bring something new and different to the YouTube astrology world or I'd get left behind. Not to mention the fact that the topic of astrology and metaphysics is not exactly supported by my cultures. My Salvadoran side had never had an issue with it, but I think that's mostly because I know better than to bring it up at family dinners. My mother and tia are both very open-minded, so I am lucky for that! My tia and I actually planned to get our tarot cards read together this month, so I know she is supportive! As for my other side, it can be considered quite taboo, if I'm being honest. If you ask a Jamaican what their sign is, they will likely kiss their teeth and change the topic. It's actually quite funny.

I remember in college, I had a group of Jamaican friends and we sat for hours discussing zodiac signs. They had no idea what any of it meant, and by the end of the conversation I had most of them believing in it! The problem is, people stay away from the topic because many times astrology is seen as blasphemy. Not only astrology, but most spiritual topics such as tarot readings, psychics, crystals, and more! If you go on YouTube, you'll probably notice that there are not many black creators doing what I do! This probably has to do with the fact that most of us weren't raised to believe in such topics. I kept my YouTube channel a secret for years! My family didn't know about it until I hit around 90,000 subscribers—and that's only because another family member found it! I was so scared of what they would think. To be honest, I could've done a lot worse. Do my parents love what I do? Probably not. Do they support it? Yes.

The truth is, I'd love to see more girls that look like me on YouTube talking about zodiac signs, but I understand why black astrology YouTubers are few and far between. I'm very happy to be the representation for spiritual black women that I look for when scrolling through the internet. I know that when I look up any type of spiritual topic on YouTube, I gravitate toward the thumbnails filled with POC! I want to give some love to some of my favorite POC spiritual/astrology YouTubers that I believe deserve recognition! If you picked up this book, you will definitely love them!

- ✧   Shonetta's Divine Tarot
- ✧   Kahlen Barry
- ✧   AstroKit
- ✧   Ambitious Jemz Astrology
- ✧   Itsbabyj1
- ✧   Water Star Vibes

Lastly, I just want to say thank you. If you bought this book, that means you are supporting me on this journey. Thank you for allowing me to be the representation that I love to see in others, and thank you for letting me be with you on this journey (even if it's just as a little voice in your head as you read these pages.). Thank you for reading this book, and giving this method a chance. I've come a long way, and so will you.

Thank you.
I love you.
You got this.
Now, go be amazing!

With love,
Ashley Small-Flores

About the Author

Ashley Flores is a self-taught astrologist. You can keep up with her teachings and life on her YouTube channel, the Amateur Guru. She currently resides in Canada.

Mango Publishing, established in 2014, publishes an eclectic list of books by diverse authors—both new and established voices—on topics ranging from business, personal growth, women's empowerment, LGBTQ studies, health, and spirituality to history, popular culture, time management, decluttering, lifestyle, mental wellness, aging, and sustainable living. We were recently named 2019 *and* 2020's #1 fastest growing independent publisher by *Publishers Weekly.* Our success is driven by our main goal, which is to publish high quality books that will entertain readers as well as make a positive difference in their lives.

Our readers are our most important resource; we value your input, suggestions, and ideas. We'd love to hear from you—after all, we are publishing books for you!

Please stay in touch with us and follow us at:

Facebook: Mango Publishing
Twitter: @MangoPublishing
Instagram: @MangoPublishing
LinkedIn: Mango Publishing
Pinterest: Mango Publishing

Sign up for our newsletter at www.mangopublishinggroup.com and receive a free book!

Join us on Mango's journey to reinvent publishing, one book at a time.